Anne Hooper's
Ultimate
Sexual
Touch

ANNE HOOPER'S

ULTIMATE
SEXUAL
TOUCH

A Lover's Guide to Sex through Sensuality

DORLING KINDERSLEY
London • New York • Stuttgart

A DORLING KINDERSLEY BOOK

Created and produced by
CARROLL & BROWN LIMITED
5 Lonsdale Road
London NW6 6RA

Project Editor Ian Wood

Art Editor Sally Powell
Designers Carmel O'Neill,
Karen Sawyer

Photography Jules Selmes

Production Wendy Rogers
Amanda Mackie

First published in Great Britain in 1995
by Dorling Kindersley Limited,
9 Henrietta Street, London WC2E 8PS

A CIP catalogue record for this book is available from the
British Library.

ISBN 0 7513 0176 0

Reproduced by Colourscan, Singapore
Printed in EU Officine Grafiche De Agostini – Novara 1995

CONTENTS

INTRODUCTION

One of the first questions I am invariably asked by new friends and acquaintances is, "Why did you become a sex therapist?" The honest answer is, "Because I enjoy sex." Sex has been a source of fun, happiness, play – everything that's positive in my life. I think now I was lucky. I was blessed with parents who were sensual with each other and loving toward their offspring. And I was also lucky with my early menfriends, who joined uninhibitedly in my exploration of sex and sensuality.

It was only later that I understood that the discovery of sensuality and sex wasn't the same for everyone. There were people who didn't spontaneously find their sexuality. As I grew older, I became motivated to help men and women grasp the experience I'd been so fortunate to find for myself. That is when I decided to train as a sex therapist, and since then, I've learned how important it is to help people at the earliest stages of their relationships – hence my books on sexuality. My interest in

sex therapy began in the 1970s. Sex therapy as such didn't exist in the UK in those days, although some brave and pioneering individuals were struggling to develop their own methods.

DISCOVERING SEXUALITY
Most people discover their sexuality quite spontaneously, but others need more time to learn about it – or to be taught about it.

In the USA, however, programmes for training and retraining adults in all aspects of sexuality were being researched, formulated, and put into practice. Thanks to the interest that American academics showed in the study of human sexuality, the USA became the world leader in the development of therapeutic help for people with sexual difficulties.

MASSAGE TRAINING

My first serious exposure to sensual massage was at the hands of a massage trainer employed by the then newly formed Institute for the Advanced Study of Human Sexuality, in San Francisco. This was the first American organization licensed to award a degree in sexology. The Institute, while encouraging important research work and serious theses from its students, also included a great deal of "bodywork" among both students and clients.

Just off the foyer of the Institute, at the times I visited, was a huge redwood tub that acted as a communal bath. At regular periods during the working day, the various principals of the establishment could be seen inside it, taking a comfortable break alongside any of the junior staff who had the time and were similarly inclined. There were no status barriers, no inhibitions about nudity, and many of the students' workshops were focused specifically on gaining and receiving good sensual touch.

GIVING REASSURANCE
In the early stages of a relationship, you may need to guide and reassure your partner if he or she is unsure how to respond to touch.

I learned a lot just from being in the presence of these individuals; the main lesson being how to be comfortable with sexuality. For a sex therapist this is, not surprisingly, just about the most important ability to acquire. If you aren't comfortable thinking and talking about sex, there is no way your clients can be, either. Your discomfort is a barrier to exploring their problems.

This sense of comfort with sex was further enriched by meeting Betty Dodson and taking part in her "bodysex" workshops. She is a remarkable role model and an inspiration, and it's thanks to her that I started my English Women's Sexuality Workshop and wrote my book (*The Body Electric*) about a fictional group of women who might have taken part in one of my courses. Further inspiration came,

although indirectly, from US therapist Lonnie Barbach. The group methods Lonnie used for working with preorgasmic women were models for the groups I set up in the UK.

THERAPY AND TOUCH

If you are wondering why I am relating how body-oriented sex therapy methods originated in the USA, it is because I want to illustrate the unusual (by today's standards) influences that shaped my own background as a sex therapist. While pioneering the women's sexuality groups in the UK, I was also training in the behavioural methods of sex education at the first English sex therapy clinic. These methods were pioneered by

Masters and Johnson and used experimentally by doctors, psychiatrists, and psychologists. The "sensate focus" techniques (sensual pleasuring under another name) were adapted to be more acceptable to the English culture, but remained in essence much the same. The UK therapists differed from early US practitioners in developing the personal counselling aspect much further, so that couples had the chance to study their relationships in great depth while developing their sensate focusing techniques.

The common denominator in all the methods and experiences described is touch: perfectly gorgeous and undemanding caresses and strokes, neither pressurizing nor pressurized – fingertip magic. The more I worked with men and women who had difficulties in bed, the more I realized the great value of laying fingers on skin. There is no doubt that doing bodywork, either in a group or between couples, speeds up the impact of any counselling. Experience made it clear to me that good touch cultivates friendship and enhances warmth. The easier you find it to touch, the greater the comfort you bring to a partner's skin; the more you can provoke and accept a partner's sensual reaction, the more likely you are to develop a sound relationship.

BUILDING UP FEELINGS

This book is thus about more than safe sex. The slow, sensuous build-up of bodily feeling can evolve into an intense concentration of emotional feeling. At the very least, sensual

BUILDING TRUST
Finding out about each other's responses to touch will help you and your partner to build mutual trust.

touch engenders a warm sense of friendship. At most, for a few people on rare but wonderful occasions, it can amount to a spiritual experience. That may sound like an exaggerated claim, but I know, from my own experiences and those reported to me by my clients and friends, that it happens. I suspect, though, that it can only do so when the touch is given by a lover, and possibly this has to be a very special lover whose presence alone heightens all your feelings.

Although this book focuses mainly on learning and practising the touching skills, it is not confined to non-penetrative sex. Yes, a scintillating massage can be a delightful alternative to intercourse, but it can also be used as a stimulating adjunct to it. For me, sexual intercourse is an all-over body experience that includes penetration, but if I don't get a great deal of touching and teasing, caressing, hugging, and occasionally some games-playing before intercourse, I feel short-changed. I also feel less aroused, and find it harder to achieve orgasm without these.

My preferences are not necessarily going to be the same as other people's. There are some people who adore the straightforwardness of intercourse and need no other stimulation. There are others (some women) who feel violated by penetration but respond enthusiastically to stimulation by hand. Men, whose sexuality is often focused on the penis, do not necessarily want only this part of their body stimulated, and research on homosexual lovemaking has shown that male couples go in for a great deal of all-over body stimulation.

I think that erotic touch is one of the major gifts of our lives, and that students of sensual massage are likely to be among the greatest of lovers. I hope sincerely that the skills that lie at your fingertips will be nurtured and encouraged when you practise the strokes and try the erotic encounter suggestions that lie within these pages. Happy touching!

CONFIDENCE
Learning about your sexual reponses will help you to increase your self-confidence.

ABOUT THIS BOOK

In this book, I have set out to show how you and your partner can develop your sensuality. By doing so, you will learn how to experience all those heart-stopping aspects of touch that can be so arousing. Of course, it's marvellous if you can find this out for yourself, without any assistance from books. But if you aren't sure how to go about it, or if you'd like to pick up a few ideas to help you on your way, this book is for you.

Sensual touch can be enjoyed by people who are just good friends, as well as by lovers, and it can establish lasting bonds of friendship. The first two chapters of this book, therefore, deal with establishing trustworthiness and defining the ground rules, for which, in this instance, read "agreeing not to make touch sexual".

For those of you who are lovers (or who intend to be), the third chapter tells you how to extend your touch from the friendly to the sexual. It explains how you can increase your sexual responses, and describes male and female sexual anatomy, arousal, and orgasm.

Essential information
The first chapters of the book marshal all the research and facts you need to help you understand your body and that of your partner.

MASSAGE AND AROUSAL
At the core of the book are the chapters on massage. The first of these shows you the best techniques to use for a sensual body massage, and this is followed by a description of highly arousing genital massage strokes. The third massage chapter is a guide to self-touch, a type of massage that is pleasurable in itself and also teaches you a lot about your body's sensual responses.

Our attitudes to physical arousal, our desire for it, and our responses to it can be greatly influenced by major events in our lives, such as pregnancy, the arrival

Practical instruction
The pages on the practical techniques of sensual body massage are fully illustrated and take you step by step through each stroke.

Case history boxes give examples of individual experiences that illustrate the general theme of the text

Tint boxes provide useful additional information that complements the main text

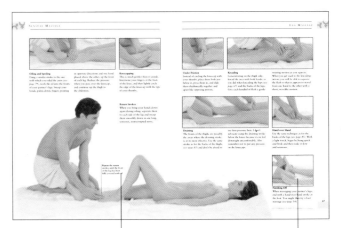

Annotations highlight important areas of the body in each exercise

Step-by-step photographic sequences show you how to give a massage

Imaginative sex

The chapter on erotic encounters provides varied and imaginative scenarios upon which to base your own sexual experimentation.

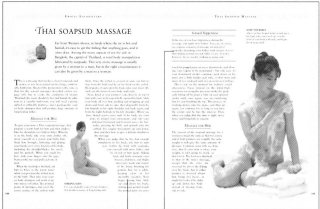

Detailed practical advice is given on setting up the scenarios and on how to use props and develop the situations

Text boxes give you further information and advice or suggest enjoyable variations on the main theme

of a new baby, the menopause, and the male mid-life crisis. The chapter on life changes explains how loving touch can help us to cope with these, and it also describes the effects of aging on sexuality. For example, young men tend to get aroused much more easily than do older men, but women may discover that their capacity for arousal and orgasm becomes much greater when they reach their thirties.

Our sexual arousal can also be affected by the state of our health, and by certain medications and drugs. In the chapter on improving the experience of sex, I describe some of the commonest

COMPLETE SENSUALITY

A proper understanding of your own sensuality and that of your partner will help you to build a strong and lasting relationship.

examples of factors that reduce or prevent sexual response – and how they can be avoided or their effects minimized. I also explain how sexual response can be heightened by the use of sexual fantasy, which is a key ingredient of the final chapter of the book.

EROTIC ENCOUNTERS

In the last chapter of the book, I show how you can spice up your love life by playing sex games, creating and even acting out your sexual fantasies, and devising erotic scenarios for lovemaking. The eight "erotic encounters" I describe will, I hope, show you how you can prevent the sexual side of your relationship from becoming predictable and boring.

MAKING CONTACT

 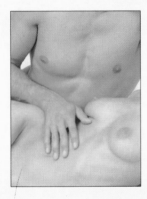 

The giving and receiving of touch is an
integral part of any physical relationship. How
an individual reacts to being touched depends
largely upon his or her previous experiences,
and this is something that you should take
into account when beginning a relationship
with a new partner.

EACH OTHER'S SKIN

Most of us fail to give our skin a second thought. It's just there – the covering that protects the inner flesh from the outside air. Yet the skin is a human being's biggest sex organ, and it also provides us with a direct route to each other's emotions.

LOVING TOUCH
The feelings of warmth and intimacy engendered by tender, loving touch will help your relationship to grow deeper and stronger.

If we are excited or sad, angry or hopeful, the emotions will surface when our lovers lay hands on us. This is because a basic type of sensuality is planted within us when we are babies. What that sensuality consists of depends on the quality of touch we received when we were tiny. If that touch was good, our maturing feelings will grow into a happy enjoyment of sensuality, but if it was bad, our adult response to touch will probably become aggressive rejection.

We know this because of some famous experiments carried out on monkeys in the 1950s. Orphaned baby monkeys that had been raised with cuddly, cloth, surrogate mothers showed few behavioural problems when they grew up, but those raised with-

Many parts of the head, including the earlobes, lips, and throat, are highly sensitive to touch

The hands and fingers play a key role in sensual touch by both giving and receiving tactile sensation

out surrogates turned out to be aggressive and rejecting when they matured. And when the females became mothers, they had no idea how to be maternal, and were either indifferent or, in some cases, violent to their young. Those that had been deprived of sensual input as babies could not give sensual output as adults.

And much as I would hate to suggest that human beings are remotely like rats, the fact remains that some of the research on rats may also have relevance to our species. In the 1950s, an American survey compared 20 rats that were petted with 20 others that were not. The petted rats learned faster and grew faster. If this work can be related to humans, we may assume that the more we are stroked as infants, the more we will learn and progress as adults.

TOUCH AND SURVIVAL

Going even further, Dr James Prescott, an American neuropsychologist, theorized that human violence often stems from a lack of bodily pleasure during the formative periods of life. Laboratory experiments convinced him that rage is not possible in the presence of pleasure, and he has stated that deprivation of sensory pleasure is a major ingredient in the expression of physical violence.

In fact, touch turns out to be a vital part of survival. Baby animals are almost literally licked into shape immediately after

birth. With some species, if this isn't done, the babies die almost immediately. And research shows that good skin nourishment – touching and stroking – might provide us with the will to live.

This idea was first put forward by Dr René Spitz, of the New York Foundling Hospital, after a holiday in Mexico. In what was something of a busman's holiday, he visited a local orphanage. He was surprised by the appearance of the resident babies because they were in so much better health than those of his own establishment. They also appeared to be happier. In New York, the babies, although clean and well fed, had a high death rate.

On making some inquiries, he learned that local women visited the Mexican orphanage every day and played with the babies. In New York, however, the babies were hardly touched and spent most of their time alone in their cots. This discovery inspired Dr Spitz to instigate a famous study, which confirmed that regular touch is not just life-enhancing but is necessary for healthy survival.

MEMORIES OF TOUCH

Touch, therefore, brings with it memories. In order to enjoy wonderful touch with a partner now, it helps to know what touch meant to that partner when he or she was a baby. Gaining an understanding of our own touch histories is also a good idea.

Skin sensitivity
Some areas are more sensitive than others because they contain more nerve endings, very closely packed together. For instance, the fingertips, where the nerves are densely packed, are much more sensitive to touch than the skin of the back.

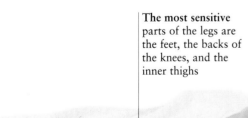

The most sensitive parts of the legs are the feet, the backs of the knees, and the inner thighs

CASE HISTORY
FRANCESCA AND TOUCH DEPRIVATION

As a tiny child, Francesca was deprived of loving touch and was frequently slapped, locked in cupboards, or just ignored. As an adult, she was terribly needy for loving touch: she couldn't get enough of it. She was a good mother herself, cuddling and hugging her children and bringing them up, as a deserted single parent, to the highest possible standards. She later learned that her constant craving for touch from her husband (who had found it hard to keep up with her needs) was really a result of her very deprived childhood.

RELATIONSHIP PROBLEMS

A more complicated problem emerges when you have been in a sexual relationship for some time – perhaps it has been successful in terms of orgasms but it still manages to leave you disappointed. Passion doesn't fit into the picture anywhere. Neither you nor your partner has yet worked out that passion (or the lack of it) has everything to do with how we give and receive touch. Touch isn't just a matter of hands on bodies; it's also a state of mind. By awakening our early memories, we may (no promises, alas) be able to expand the spiritual side of touch.

The "up" side of connecting through touch is that it acts as a shortcut to a person's innermost sensual character. Anna said of her new lover, "I'd known David for years, as a friend – a nice, trustworthy, dull friend. Shortly after my marriage broke up he took me out to dinner so I could cry on his shoulder – which I did. But after the meal, he held my hand when we walked to the car and I felt as though an electric current was surging through me.

EXPLORATION
When exploring each other's bodies, you are helping to build mutual trust while giving and receiving sensual pleasure.

As well as using your hands, caress your partner's skin with your lips, tongue, and hair (if it's long enough)

When your partner caresses you, close your eyes so that your sense of being touched is heightened

Make sure that your fingernails are not sharp or broken

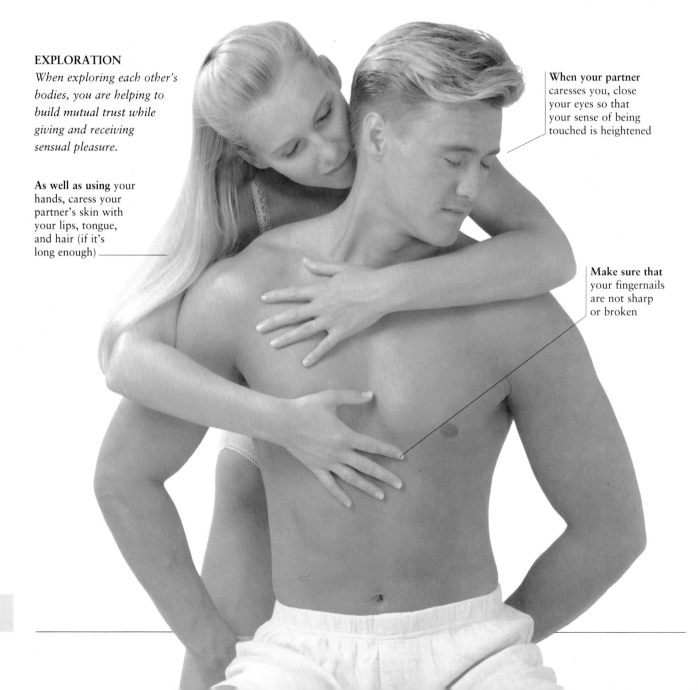

I could suddenly feel things about his sensuality, and therefore about him, that I'd had no idea existed.

"Four years on, he still has only to touch me and I'm instantly connected to this marvellous inner man. It's truly exciting, knowing that such an intensely sensual human being is wrapped up in this seemingly ordinary exterior."

CULTURAL DIFFERENCES

European men and women touch each other conspicuously more than their North American counterparts. A touch survey showed that American friends touched two to three times an hour while Europeans touched on average 100 times an hour. Our culture, therefore, even literally the land we are born into, will affect our attitudes to touch and our experiences of it. If friendly touch is rarer in America than in Southern Europe, for example, it's fair to suppose that it has a different significance to Americans than to Europeans.

Where touch may offer Europeans feelings of security, Americans could feel threatened by it. Establishing your good intentions at the beginning of a relationship may turn out to be far more important in the United States than in, for example, France. Which isn't to say that good intentions aren't *always* important – they are. Getting these across before laying a loving finger on a potential partner is a practical rule of thumb!

ASKING QUESTIONS

I hope I've made the case for finding out about your partner's first experiences of touch, what kind of a role touch played in his or her early family life, and what circumstances the family lived in. This is information that will allow your relationship to expand mentally and emotionally while your skin – and that of your partner – becomes increasingly responsive to wonderful sensation.

The Touch Questionnaire below is designed to help you and your partner find out about each other's experience of touch. The questions are aimed at stirring the memory and providing you with hitherto stored information. There are no right or wrong answers.

THE TOUCH QUESTIONNAIRE

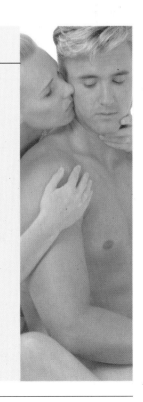

Earliest Recollections
- *What are your earliest recollections of being lovingly touched?*
- *What are your earliest recollections of being punishingly touched?*
- *What are your earliest recollections of touching someone?*
- *What are your first memories of sensual feeling?*
- *Which member or members of your family cuddled you regularly?*
- *Did you have a security blanket or other comfort object as a baby?*
- *What are your earliest recollections of the textures you slept in?*
- *What are your earliest recollections of the textures you were clothed in?*

Childhood
- *Did you sleep alone or with someone?*
- *If you slept with someone, what do you remember of physical contact?*
- *Did you play touch games as a child?*
- *If you did, what was your parents' attitude to this?*
- *Did you caress yourself as a child?*
- *If you did, what was your parents' attitude to this?*
- *Were you physically close to your best friends?*
- *If you were, what attitude did others take to this?*
- *As a child, did you cuddle your parents?*
- *Did they cuddle you?*
- *How old were you when this stopped?*

THE EARLY STAGES

Part of the natural life "task" of adolescents is to separate from their parents in order to establish themselves as independent beings. They need to accomplish this both for their own sakes and for those of their parents. As part of this separation, the cuddles and caresses between parents and child usually stop. This, in turn, means that the young person craves sensual input.

The reason children withdraw physically from their parents is the burgeoning of sexual feeling. Their biological clocks send a flood of sex hormones into the bloodstream, and touch that was previously sensual now has a sexual element in it. Loving touch suddenly needs to be directed toward a lover, or at least someone with the potential to be a lover.

Use reassuring touch to encourage your partner to confide in you

LISTEN AND RESPOND
When you are learning about a new partner's sensual history, listen to what he or she has to say and respond to it. Be ready to shift your angle of questioning if you sense that your partner is unwilling to follow the existing line.

Respond to your partner's disclosures by telling him or her your own story – the conversation should not be one-sided

Before you become a lover, however, it is important to find out as much as you can about the object of your desires. My Touch Questionnaire (*see page 17*) is an example of one way in which you can begin to find out about your partner's background. At its best, it provides invaluable knowledge of the other's sensual history. Applied to ourselves, it also gives us an insight into our own. But pitfalls can open up along the way of these early disclosures.

For example, your partner may be afraid to reveal crucial details of his or her early life because they include an episode of abuse or even incest. To help offload these distressing recollections, your partner may need to hear you say you will not be disgusted or repelled by anything he or she is going to say. In order to do that, you need first to find out what reaction it is that they most dread. The conversation might go:

You: *"What is it that scares you most?"*
Partner: *"I'm afraid you'll think I'm awful, that you won't like me anymore."*
You: *"I promise you that you won't shock me, that nothing you can say will alter me liking you, and that if you're going to feel bad I'll do everything I can to make you feel better."*

A word of warning – you need to examine your intentions before making these promises, because having made them, you've got to stick to them. If you think that you can't follow through, you should refrain from promising. Indeed, this would be the time to call a halt to the proceedings because your partner could be deeply upset were you to let him or her down.

A PARTNER'S DISTRESS

Your permission to disclose might unleash a storm. For example, it can be very moving to talk about an episode of abuse, which perhaps has never been brought out before. Be prepared to do a great deal of sympathizing, comforting, and just listening. It might be necessary to delay the rest of the exercise until another occasion.

If your partner, having revealed a deep secret, is distressed and cannot recover, and you feel out of your depth, continue to be warm and supportive but help him or her find a professional counsellor to consult as soon as possible. Encourage your partner to go for this assistance, offer to go as well if that seems a good idea, and offer support while he or she tries to come to terms with this negative experience.

Be patient
If your partner is very hesitant, take it slowly and give him or her gentle encouragement. Be prepared to go back to some of the key questions later, and do not expect immediate answers to them.

DEALING WITH YOUR OWN NERVOUSNESS

• If you are nervous, ask for reassurance. If you don't get any, don't feel guilty about saying you do not feel quite ready for such an experiment yet.

• Take note of your own body language. If you realize that you are tense, try to relax by breathing quietly but deeply and evenly, letting your muscles go limp.

• Pay attention to your own feelings of resistance. Such feelings often arise because we consider anything sexual to be valid only if it is spontaneous. From my clinical experience, I know that there are many aspects of relationships that need to be learned, precisely because they have not happened spontaneously. These include sexual moves and self-revelation.

• If you are convinced that it is important for you to be frank, but you are not sure that you will find the courage, use the Yes/No Assertion Exercise. In this, you say "Yes" to things that you feel convinced are right for you, and "No" to things that are not. It is possible to practice this on quite simple dilemmas or on very serious problems. It is an exercise that lets you work out your priorities and act on them.

USING PERSONAL DISCLOSURE

Your partner's problem may not, of course, be as deep-seated as child abuse but be something rather more common, such as inhibition. It can be difficult for someone who is very shy and inexperienced to talk matter-of-factly about sex, especially when it is his own sex life that is under scrutiny. Taking the lead here by personal example may be helpful. For example, you might say: "It's hard to reveal everything, isn't it? I can see for myself that it's a good idea, but I feel quite inhibited. I hope you'll bear with me if I seem a bit slow at talking."

From there on, you do need to let your partner hear something about yourself. In this way you are revealing yourself to be as vulnerable as he or she is. You are also showing by example that it is possible to ask for understanding and encouragement. This makes it easier should your partner wish to ask for your patience.

DEALING WITH ANGER

It is unlikely, but possible, that during your delvings into the past, your partner will unleash a lot of anger caused by previous events never before properly dealt with. Being faced with someone in a towering, shimmering rage can be daunting, especially if it was you who prompted it and it seems to be directed against you. The first thing to remember is that such rage has nothing to do with your questions: it stems from past events.

The second is to force yourself to see beyond your partner's outburst and let him or her get on with being angry, instead of trying to cut off the rage by your own self-defence. The sooner your partner can get the anger out of his or her system, the sooner he or she will calm down. Part of this process lies in helping your partner to work out who it was, in the past, that caused the anger.

Signs of Nervousness
The woman's nervousness is revealed by her body language. He has adopted a posture that mirrors hers.

Following Her Lead
She has shifted her position. He is mirroring it, hoping to establish an unconscious link in her mind between her posture and his.

USING BODY LANGUAGE

Pay attention to body language. If your partner appears keen on talking things through, but then sits with legs and arms tightly crossed, it's likely that this is a sign of nervousness. If this happens, try the technique known as "mirroring" *(see below)*, which is an interesting way of altering your partner's body language and mood at the same time.

Sit opposite your partner and adopt (inconspicuously) a similar body pose. For example, if your partner's arms are crossed, follow suit, and if he or she shifts position, shift yours to match. Once your partner has had a chance to take in and mimic (unconsciously) your body position, slowly start to alter it. On most occasions, your partner's body posture will shift to match yours. In this way, it is possible to unwind your partner and get him or her to sit in a more relaxed fashion.

ESTABLISHING TRUST

The desirability of establishing trust, of becoming trustworthy, of not rushing the sexual side of a partnership, has many obvious parallels in the forming of personal relationships in general. A good relationship benefits from all of these, and if you want to make solid friendships, you might do worse than learn how to do so through sensual, but non-sexual, massage exercise. In addition to massage exercise, non-sexual beginnings to any good relationship might include:
• affectionately putting an arm around your friend
• hugging briefly
• holding hands
• all tentative activities that establish the degree to which contact is acceptable.

Initiating a Change
He has started to alter his posture, making it more open. She has responded by matching his new position.

Openness and Trust
He has successfully used the technique of mirroring to overcome her nervousness, and now she feels that she can confide in him.

PLAYING *with* TOUCH

Playful, exploratory touch games help to
nurture the physical side of a new relationship,
and provide an enjoyable introduction to the
pleasures of massage. You can also use them
to revitalize an established relationship if
either (or both) of you feels that your
lovemaking has lost its sparkle.

TOUCH PLAY

One of the joyous aspects of falling in love is the rediscovery of the child within us. Suddenly it feels right to laugh and play, mess around and tumble, flirt and provoke. For many of us this happens quite naturally, and it's a wonderful way to discover what spontaneity and life our lover draws from within us.

Stress relief
The symptoms of stress often include muscular tension. By relaxing the muscles, massage helps the mind to relax and so helps to create a feeling of contentment.

As real children, of course, we play too, for the same reasons and with the same results. We learn about the world and the people around us, and touch plays a huge part in this very personal education.

Even if we weren't deliberately massaged as babies, most of us learned to enjoy touch while we were being handled, fondled, played with, bounced, petted, cuddled, and caressed – but not all, unfortunately. Some of us, with cold, undemonstrative parents, were deprived of this vital start.

Here is one example. Ian had received very little affectionate cuddling and stroking from his mother as a baby, and what little he did receive ceased as soon as breastfeeding ended. In later life, he "armoured" himself with rigidly held muscles. These rigid muscles are a defence – a defence against feeling untouched and unloved. Giving someone like Ian a simple massage could be difficult to begin with because, to him, a soft touch will feel irritating rather than pleasurable.

A different case is Jane's. When she was a child, she was told constantly by her parents that she was ugly (which was untrue), and physically rebuffed by her father every time she tried to snuggle close to him. Because of this continual denigration and rejection in childhood, by the time she reached adulthood she had very little self-esteem. She found it terrifying even to think about getting close to a partner, let alone allowing it to happen. Her response to loving touch was fear.

LEARNING POSITIVE RESPONSES

Both Ian and Jane found that because they had received no loving touch while they were growing up, they were unable to respond to it as adults. Knowledge of touch, which seems patently obvious to those of us who were fortunate enough to have had sensual mothers and fathers, won't even exist in the minds of those who were play- and skin-starved.

The good news is that even if we haven't had too much good touching as infants, we can still take in good touch at a later age. Indeed, this can go further. By learning positive responses to being touched, we can actually develop new neural pathways in the brain and catch up on experiencing good sensuality. So embarking on a series of touch games is a way of feeding information into our brains that we can use when appropriate. We can expand our knowledge and our range of sensual experience in this way.

SOCIALIZING EFFECTS

We now know, through work with autistic children, that it is possible to introduce a human being to touch experience in order to change his or her perception of the world. The logical conclusion is that we may still be able to socialize unruly adults with some intense touch experience. Being kissed, cuddled, and stroked as babies is therefore vital to how responsive as partners we are in later life.

TUNING IN TO MOODS

Different sorts of touch suit different sorts of occasions. If a friend's parent has just died, it is all right to hold him or her and offer comfort with your physical presence. It obviously would not be an appropriate moment to suggest stripping off for a sensual massage. And someone who is very angry will be irritated rather than calmed if you suggest playing touch games.

So always take the trouble to find out how your friend is feeling. But do note that massage can be highly beneficial, emotionally as well as physically, and it has been known to lift depression.

BENEFITS OF TOUCH

Many people have benefited greatly from being introduced (or reintroduced) to the experience of touch, particularly in the form of massage. I well remember one young woman in a women's group who was severely depressed, to the point of feeling suicidal. Letting herself be touched in the group massage, and discovering how good and comforting this felt, was her starting point for recovery. The warm, non-threatening physical contact that it entailed helped her to feel valued and less isolated. This in turn increased her self-esteem and self-confidence, which gave her new hope for the future.

In the late 1970s in part of North London, elderly men and women who were given regular massage by a visiting social worker declared that the quality of their lives had radically improved. And during this same period, at St Albans' Hill End Hospital, England, disturbed teenagers were put through a concentrated programme of touching and being touched. As a result, the level of violence among them became markedly lower.

MASSAGE

Even those of us who did get a lot of play and tumble as babies, and don't "need" such massage moves in quite the same way as those who were less fortunate, are still liable to forget the value of touch. But it can be fun to be reminded of it, and for those of us who were starved of touch, massage is a terrific way of catching up on the good sensations we have missed. And it's always worth remembering that a massage is a sensuous experience for the person giving it as well as for the recipient.

LOVE AND PLAY

It is no accident that partners play together at the beginning of a new love affair – it is through play that we learn. Play teaches us about ourselves, our emotions and reactions and those of our partner, and how relationships function through interactions. In other words, we get to know each other.

Eye contact, smiles, and gentle, loving touch help you express your feelings for each other

AGREEING THE RULES

Many readers of this book will be in established relationships that they want to extend. They will already have grown comfortable with nudity and will also have made the leap from sensual touch to sexual intercourse. In theory, then, they will possess a wealth of sensual information about each other.

Reassurance
Be ready to give your partner friendly reassurance if he or she appears nervous or uncertain.

Not all students of sensual touch, however, are yet living together or married, and there will be some who are just beginning a relationship. These are men and women who are hoping to set that new friendship off on a sensual footing, and who will be gathering sensual facts about each other along the way.

GETTING COMFORTABLE

So that both groups (those with new lovers and those with old) cover the same ground, I intend to describe the beginnings of massage and its boundaries as if none of you have yet touched each other or taken off your clothes together. Even if you feel this section is not relevant, please take a look at it. Some valuable concepts arise – for instance about putting each other at ease and creating trust and intimacy – that are valuable at any stage of any relationship, sexual or otherwise.

When learning massage for the first time, the first rule is to state firmly that it is not going to end in intercourse. I'm sorry if that disturbs the more sexually focused among you, but I hope you will understand that a wonderful massage provides a sensual alternative to intercourse. It's important to come to this agreement, because the knowledge that there will be no sexual intercourse involved affects how the massage is experienced.

This doesn't mean that at a later date, when you know your way around massage, you can't then change the rules if both of you want it and agree to it. Lovemaking, when preceded by the sort of wonderful tactile treat that a good sensual massage can provide, is especially satisfying.

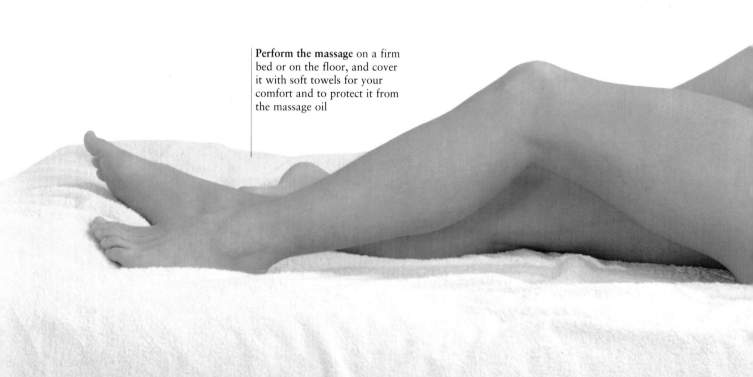

Perform the massage on a firm bed or on the floor, and cover it with soft towels for your comfort and to protect it from the massage oil

ESTABLISHING GROUND RULES

This involves explaining, at the beginning of the first massage session, what the boundaries of the massage consist of. For example, in a couple of brief sentences you might tell your partner that sexual intercourse is not part of the proceedings, that verbal feedback between the two of you is expected, and that if at any time the massagee dislikes something, he or she has only to say so for it to stop. The person who is being massaged also, of course, has the option of withdrawing from the session at any time – and for any reason – if he or she chooses to do so.

THE VERSATILE MASSAGE

One of the delights of massage is that it can be used in a variety of ways and at different levels of intimacy, combining physical and emotional pleasure to varying degrees.

WHEN NOT TO MASSAGE

Despite the pleasure it gives, there are times when massage is inadvisable. Do not massage over varicose veins or recent scar tissue, and never give your partner a massage if he or she:
• has a skin infection, a fever, a contagious illness, thrombosis, phlebitis, or heart problems
• has recently undergone surgery or suffered serious injury, or has acute back or other pain
• has any severe swelling or bruising, or acute inflammation.
If in doubt, always seek medical advice.

Intimacy
Relaxing together after a massage is a great way to prolong the feelings of intimacy that it creates.

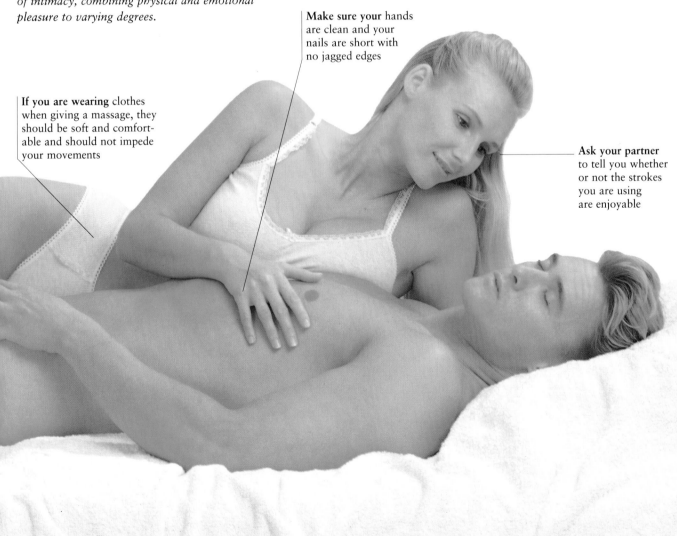

Make sure your hands are clean and your nails are short with no jagged edges

If you are wearing clothes when giving a massage, they should be soft and comfortable and should not impede your movements

Ask your partner to tell you whether or not the strokes you are using are enjoyable

BEGINNING THE MASSAGE

Massage is a more structured activity than getting to know a friend. Making the introductory moves into a deliberate ritual allows them to become more acceptable while, at the same time, gives each of you the opportunity to feel comfortable about touching.

When you are going to give a massage, always lay out in advance any equipment you need, such as oil and towels. Keep the lights dim and ensure you have absolute privacy, but if one of you is nervous, ask a friend to be in a nearby room.

Start by carrying out a simple beginning ceremony. Sit cross-legged in front of each other, without touching, and practise deep breathing in unison. Breathe in through the nose for a count of four, and then out through the mouth for a count of four. Do this for five minutes. Then, each of you carry out the following exercise routine.

For a count of three, rotate your head slowly from side to side, extending it forward then backward so that the bones in your neck are loosened. Then, for a count of four, rotate both shoulders at the same time, first forward and then backward,

stretching them as far as they will go in each direction so that they loosen up and the arm sockets feel exercised.

Next, stretch your arms out in front of you as far as they will go, with the backs of the hands facing each other. Windmill them slowly in circles, stretching as far to the side as you can reach while turning them so that the backs of the hands are now turned completely outward.

On the inward turn, drop your arms down to your side, still stretching them and with the palms of your hands facing up. Then move them slowly into position in front of your body. As they reach the front, turn them back so that the backs of the hands once again face each other. Repeat the sequence slowly, three times. This exercises all the bones in the arm and rotates the arms in their sockets.

Now rotate your hands so that the wrist bones are exercised, wriggling your fingers to loosen them at the same time. Do this quite fast, for a count of 10.

Then stretch down from the waist toward the floor, first to the left, then to the right, as if you were trying to touch the floor to the side. This exercises the muscles

SENSUAL SURROUNDINGS

A massage is a sensual experience, so the surroundings should emphasize sensuality. The skin tenses when it is cold and is likely to experience touch as painful. When the skin is warm, the whole body relaxes and touch is experienced as pleasure. You must therefore ensure that the room is very warm and that your massaging hands are, too.

Clothing
For the person giving the massage, loose, light clothing, affording maximum move-ment and a sense of freedom, is ideal. Take

off any rings and other jewellery you might be wearing, because these can catch on your partner's skin or hair.

Cleanliness
Scrupulous cleanliness is important, and clean hands are essential because even a tiny grain of dirt on the hand can be experienced as a piece of sharp grit when it is rubbed over the skin during massage. If you are the one giving the massage, wash your hands in hot water before you begin.

at the side of the waist and stretches the spine where it pivots in the pelvic girdle.

Standing on one leg and holding on to something for support, draw the other up with your foot as tight against the back of your upper thigh as possible, and then stretch it out in front of you several times. Exercise first one leg, then the other, to tone up the muscles and exercise the knee joints. To exercise your ankle joints, stand on one leg, point the other in front of you, and rotate the foot first in clockwise and then in anticlockwise circles. Repeat on the other foot, each time for a count of ten.

Finally, exercise the muscles of your face. Screw it up as hard as possible, grimacing to stretch your mouth. Hold for a count of five, and then let go and relax.

RELAXING TOGETHER

Lie side by side, flat on your backs, and consciously relax. This may be difficult if either of you is not used to it, or is feeling self-conscious. To help you relax, try to empty your minds of any intrusive thoughts, and breathe slowly and deeply.

Then, using the tense/relax exercise, work your way through your limbs once more, this time focusing on muscle tension. To do this simple exercise, exaggerate the tension in each limb in turn by clenching the muscles for a count of three. Then let go and relax for a further count of three. When you feel your body is fully relaxed, just lie still and rest for about five minutes.

Massage oil
Before you begin the massage, rub warm massage oil into your hands. Apply a liberal coating to the area of your partner's skin you are going to massage.

FIRST TOUCH
When you are both relaxed, establish physical contact by affection- ate touch and holding hands.

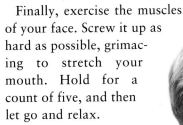

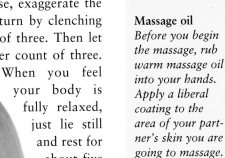

Adopt a relaxed, open pos- ture and make friendly eye contact with your partner to foster an atmosphere of trust and intimacy

Use warmth moves, such as putting a hand gently on your partner's shoulder or waist, to overcome any nervousness

Sit or kneel in a comfortable position

MASSAGE GAMES

In California, where I did some of my sex therapy training, most therapists use simple touch games to help their clients relax and become more intimate. Because we learn through play, here and on the following pages is a series of massage games that are non-sexual, non-threatening, and fun.

The famous Indian sex manual, the *Kama Sutra*, makes frequent reference to shampooing. This was a type of massage service provided to wealthy Indian men by eunuchs, and by women of low caste who were also valued for their sexual services. In ancient India, shampooing was a skilled craft, and it is on this sensuous art that the pleasurable touch game shown opposite is based.

CLOSING THE THIRD EYE

This is a wonderful starter to any session of massage games, and it consists of gentle strokes that concentrate on the "third eye", the energy centre on the forehead above the nose and the gap between the eyebrows. Your partner lies face up, and you kneel at his or her head.

Begin by resting your palms on either side of your partner's head, with your fingertips meeting at the "third eye". Hold your hands there for a minute or two of light yet enclosing touch. Then place your right palm on your partner's forehead, put your left palm on top of it, and press down firmly but gently, with gradually increasing pressure, for about ten seconds. Release slowly, eventually lifting your palms from your partner's forehead, and then repeat the stroke several times.

SCALP MASSAGE
Run your fingers through your partner's hair, and use your fingertips to massage the scalp and the back of the neck.

Sit or kneel at your partner's side

Lean across your partner and use your hand to support and balance yourself

THE SENSUAL SHAMPOO

This is ideally carried out with your friend or partner sitting up, and leaning back with head tilted back over the end of a chair or of a bath, preferably with adequate padding between the chair (or bath) and the neck. The ground below should be covered with towels and a bowl in which to catch the overflow.

Stand at the side of your friend, and after dampening (not soaking) the hair, apply enough of a mild shampoo to produce lather that will slide through the hair comfortably but not run off in rivulets. The secret to achieving this is to use water sparingly, adding to it only if necessary. Then give your partner a sensuous, massaging shampoo, as shown on the right.

THE DRY SHAMPOO

Some people won't want the bother of having to dry their hair after the massage and may prefer the dry version. Every stroke described for the Sensual Shampoo can be carried out on your friend's head without using any shampoo or water. Since the hair won't be slippery, however, take care to avoiding snagging or tangling the locks.

WET SHAMPOOING

1 Using both hands, work the shampoo into the scalp. Massage it lightly with your fingertips for several minutes, moving the hair around in small circles.

2 Support your partner's head with one hand, or lean it against your body, then cup your other hand on top of the head and gently rotate the scalp.

3 Take small locks of hair between the thumb and forefinger of each hand. Pull each lock gently to create pricklings of sensation in your partner's scalp.

4 Now massage the scalp again, this time using your fingertips, instead of a cupped hand, to move it around in small circles. Take care not to snag the hair.

66 Katie's Experience

Katie's earliest recollections were entirely sensual. She remembered, as a young child, the sensations created by twining the bedclothes around her, the feeling of her toy dog's fur, and preferring certain dresses because they felt soft. She could recall stroking her body and genitals at the age of four, but also remembered her mother's disapproval of these activities, and her father's reprimands. Now, at the age of 30, she felt as if she had shut herself off

from sensation. Although she was in a long-term sexual relationship, the lovemaking seemed to be mainly for her partner's benefit.

With the help of a women's group, she rediscovered the pleasures and benefits of sensual touch. She learned how to give and receive massage, and how to give herself sensual pleasure, including orgasms, without guilt. She subsequently had a very different and sensual love affair with a new partner. 99

THE DRESSMAKER'S DUMMY

In this, our first whole-body exercise, one partner lends his or her body as a completely passive object for the other to manipulate. This means, of course, that the lender must be assured that nothing will be done that could hurt or injure.

As the name suggests, in this touch game the partner who is taking the passive role is treated as if she or he were an inanimate object. When playing the part of the dummy, each of you will find that there can be great pleasure in feeling helpless.

The game takes place in two parts: in the first, the woman is the dummy, and in the second, the man takes that role.

STANDING UP

For the first stage of her turn as the dummy, the woman should stand up straight and make no movements of her own. The man's job is to experiment with his partner's versatility of movement, tilting and rotating her head and arms into a variety of positions. She may keep her clothes on, as long as they are not constricting, but she should take her shoes off. To get started, try the following moves.

The man stands on a chair behind his partner, and begins by gently rotating her head and tilting it from side to side and backward and forward *(see below)*. He then slips both hands under his partner's armpits and pulls up briefly to take some of the weight off her feet.

Now, the man should get off the chair, move it out of the way, and focus on his partner's arms. First, he should take her right hand in his right hand, and shake it up and down, gently at first and then more vigorously, then shake it from side to side, again increasing in vigour.

Next, taking each arm in turn, the man should hold her hand in his right hand, then put his left hand on the lower part of her arm and use it to turn the arm as far to the left as possible and then as far to the right. Finally, he should end this stage by bending and pulling his partner's arms, and rotating her lower arms in large circles clockwise and then anticlockwise.

Head Tilting
Begin by placing a chair behind her. Standing on the chair, take her head in both hands. Gently tilt it from side to side, then backward and forward. Don't force any movement – stop when the body itself resists your touch.

Bending the Arm
Hold her right elbow from behind with your right hand. With your left hand, bend her lower arm up against her upper arm so that it is doubled up. Then exert a firm but careful pressure with both hands. Hold for a count of three, let go, and repeat once.

The Arm Pull

Straighten out one of her arms and tug on it carefully, holding for a count of three, and then let go. Repeat once more. Replace her arm by her side and repeat the exercise on her other arm.

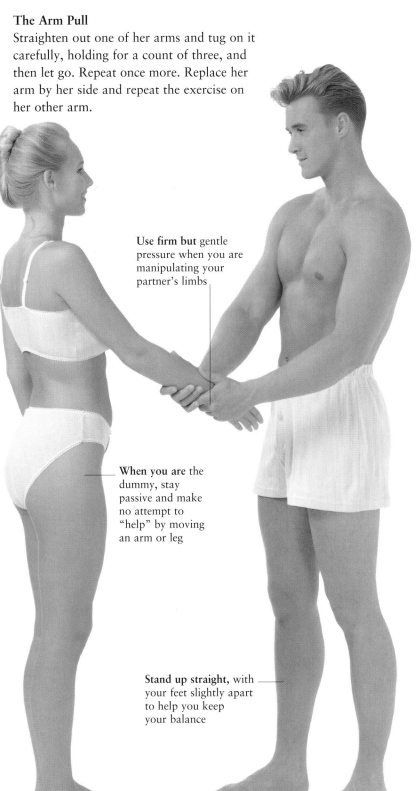

Use **firm but** gentle pressure when you are manipulating your partner's limbs

When you are the dummy, stay passive and make no attempt to "help" by moving an arm or leg

Stand up straight, with your feet slightly apart to help you keep your balance

LYING DOWN

The second stage of the game takes place with the dummy lying down. The man's job is still the same: that of playing with his partner's limbs to see what shapes he can make with her. If the woman is particularly tiny and light, the man may like to lower her gently to the ground by standing behind her and supporting her weight with his arms under her armpits.

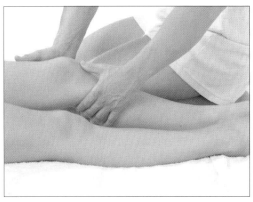

The Legs

Repeat all the arm movements, this time on each leg in turn. Don't be afraid of lifting your partner's limbs, but make sure that you do not twist them into uncomfortable positions, jerk them, or drop them suddenly.

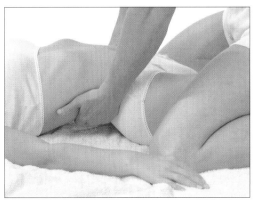

The Waist Lift

Kneel over your "dummy", lean down, put your arms around her waist, then pull her up toward you to arch her back. Hold for a count of three before lowering her back to the ground. Do not attempt this movement if your partner is heavy.

THE SENSUOUS FOOT

Feet are notoriously ticklish extremities. Many people can't bear for them to be touched at all or are insistent that a foot massage will do nothing for them. But it's worth stopping to think why the foot should be so ticklish.

According to reflexology theory, the foot plays a major role within the nervous system: every nerve in the foot (and there are many thousands) is connected up with a corresponding nerve somewhere else in the body. If you visualize every nerve in the body packed into your foot, you will get an insight into why the foot is so sensitive.

REFLEXOLOGY

Reflexologists believe that when you massage the foot, you are also, in effect, massaging the rest of the body, sending bolts of sensation and therefore energy throughout the nervous system.

FOOT MASSAGE

Equip yourself with a couple of warm, fluffy towels, some warmed massage oil, and a box of tissues in case of spills. Before beginning the massage, wash your partner's feet thoroughly in warm water and dry them carefully. Then firmly – not lightly in case of ticklishness – coat the foot with oil.

Use the strokes shown opposite. When you have finished massaging one foot, gently lower it to the ground, wrap it in a warm towel, and carry out the same massage procedure on the other foot.

Begin with gentle caresses from the lower shin to the toes

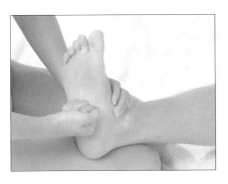

Knuckling
Hold the foot with your left hand, and press your right knuckles hard into the sole. Cover the entire sole with small circling movements.

Bending the Toes
Press the toes forward, for a count of ten, as if you were trying to bend them in the wrong direction. Repeat this three times.

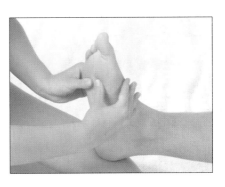

Thumbing
Work over the whole area of the sole with both thumbs simultaneously. Circle them slowly with as deep a pressure as possible.

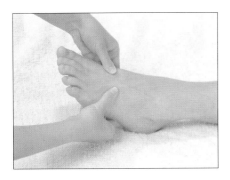

Circling
Massage the top of the foot with your thumbs, applying moderate pressure. When you near the ankle, circle with your fingertips and avoid the ankle bone itself – always avoid massaging directly on a bone.

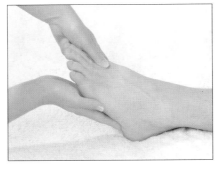

In the Grooves
The top of the foot is divided by raised tendons with grooves between them. Support the foot with one hand and, pressing firmly, run the tip of your thumb down these grooves from ankle to toe.

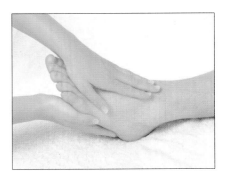

Finishing Off
Hold the foot between your hands and imagine that they are beaming energy into it. Then, very slowly, slide your hands away from the foot, pausing for a very long time before finally losing touch.

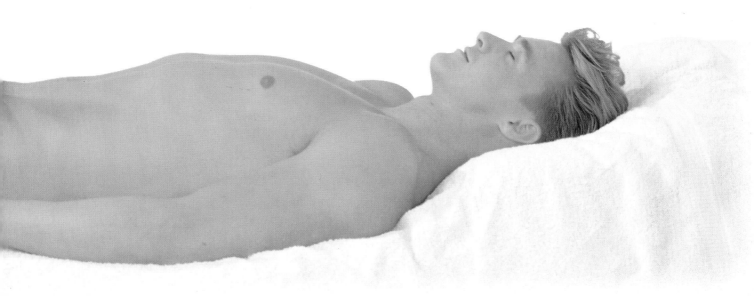

PLAYFUL MOVES

When I was taught sensual massage, I was amazed to find that we started it with a bath. It was from this and other relaxation rituals learned in my massage group that I gathered a variety of ideas which I've adapted to be enjoyed specifically by lovers.

The starting point to a massage session (and to some lovemaking sessions, of course) can be a warm dip. Floating in the bath perhaps brings back subconscious memories of floating deep inside our mothers' wombs – the most complete sensual experience we will ever know in our entire lives – where we are enclosed by sensation. Even partial immersion must revive some of those deep inner memories. After bathing, dry each other with warm, fluffy towels. Then you are ready to begin a massage, to make

love, or simply to indulge in affectionate touching such as playing with each other's hair, hugging, cuddling, kissing, and stroking each other.

PLAYING WITH HAIR

If one or both of you has long hair, playing with it can be a subtly erotic experience. Long-haired individuals can try the hair sweep, which can be curiously tantalizing. One partner (usually the man) lies flat and the long-haired one (usually the woman) covers his naked body with her locks, dragging it across the skin, sweeping it, and flicking it backward and forward. But for those of you with short locks, simply washing, combing, and brushing each other's hair, while putting the emphasis on being slow and

THE HAIR SWEEP
Let your hair hang down loosely onto his naked skin, and sweep and flick it erotically over his body and limbs.

Add to his sensations by gently blowing your hot breath onto his naked skin

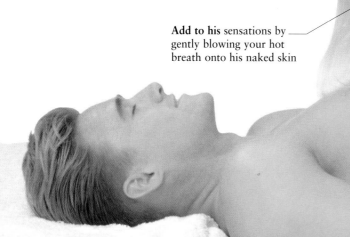

patient, can also be delightful. In fact, grooming each other in this manner can be very warm and intimate, a subtle method of getting close.

THE MAGIC MIRROR

This is a self-help exercise that can teach you to overcome any inhibitions you may have about your appearance. It involves simply looking at yourself naked in a mirror and talking about which parts of your body you like and which you dislike. For example, if you are looking in the mirror while brushing your partner's hair, make this an opportunity to reveal something of your feelings about your appearance.

Body Strokes
Take the initiative in running your hands lightly all over your partner's body, stroking it with the backs and tips of your fingers.

Warming oil
To warm up your massage oil before you begin, stand or lean the bottle in a bowl of hot water for a few minutes.

Hugging and Cuddling
Don't be afraid of hugging and cuddling. Spend hours, days, even weeks on these pleasing activities, if that feels right.

Touching Hands
Caress each other's hands, stroking them, fitting them into shapes together, massaging them, and lifting and kissing them.

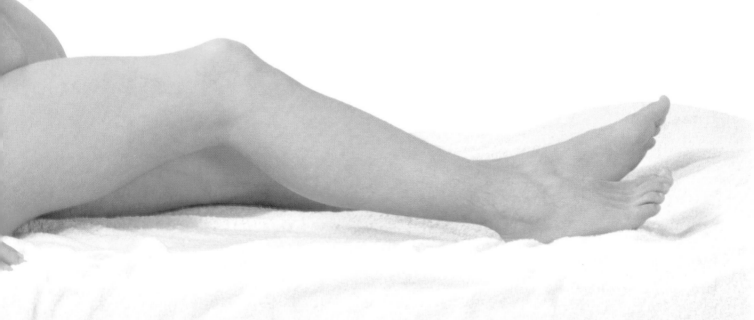

SCHOOLDAYS *in* *the* BEDROOM

Learning about your own and your partner's
sexual anatomy and responses will give you a
better understanding of the physical side of
lovemaking. This will help you to make it
more satisfying for both of you which, as well
as providing more physical pleasure, will
intensify your love for each other.

EXPLORING YOUR BODY

Many men and women have a tendency to believe that everybody has the same sexual response, but this is as incorrect as believing that all faces look the same. How you react to touch, how you experience it, and where you want to feel it, is unique to you: others' responses may be similar, but they are never the same.

It is a constant wonder to me that although we are educated for many of the things we need as adults, most of us are taught virtually nothing – other than the basics of reproduction – that is relevant to our sex lives. People in primitive societies often learned more than we do, especially if they lived in communal houses where they could actually see others making love. In many of those societies there were none of the taboos we place on sexual play for older children, and in some, the young people were paired with older ones who would initiate them into the mysteries of sex.

Yet today, school biology lessons focus first on nature, then on reproduction, and then, if you're unusually lucky, on human

reproduction – never on the physiology of pleasure. There is little likelihood of being given an explanation of your sexual response cycle, for example, or of the role of the clitoris. It would make a lot more sense if human physiology (including our sexual physiology) were studied first, and information about the birds and the bees made an optional extra.

How useful it would be to learn, for example, that hormones can influence us in many ways, not all of them benign; that diet can be responsible not just for nourishment but for our emotional well-being; that illnesses may create sexual side-effects; and that all these influences have a direct bearing on our love lives. It makes sense to give young people as good a grounding in sexual matters as possible, and yet we usually omit these most important details from formal sex education.

If I were a schoolteacher able to give my pupils a thorough preparation for their future sex lives, I would touch on several subjects. How the body functions sexually (not just reproductively); the physical

Scalp and Hair
The scalp is very sensitive to touch. It can be stimulated by direct fingertip massage, or by running your fingers through the hair.

Ears and Neck
These are among the most sensitive and erogenous parts of the body. Most people find that having their ears and neck stroked, nibbled, or licked is highly arousing, as are the sensations created by feeling a lover's hot breath in the ear.

changes we experience during arousal, orgasm, and resolution; how our bodies develop; how a healthy body may be enjoyed; and how to know when you are healthy are all vital areas of knowledge.

EROGENOUS ZONES

These and the following pages will provide you with this information about the human body and its responses. They contain the facts about male and female sexual response, plus two questionnaires. These questionnaires are based on a routine invented by American sex therapists, William Hartman and Marilyn Fithian, which aims at giving men and women detailed facts about their erogenous zones. The Sexual Body Questionnaire, for example, will provide you with knowledge of each other's skin reactions that you can put to good use when giving a sensual massage.

The value of answering these questionnaires together with your partner is that you can, in a way that provokes no feeling of criticism, let each other know what it is that you would really like. This is information you may have wanted to convey in the past but found difficult to bring out when actually in bed together.

SEXUAL BODY QUESTIONNAIRE

The aim of this questionnaire is to clarify your knowledge of each other's skin responses.
- *If making love to yourself, where would you start?*
- *How long would you spend on this?*
- *Where does your partner habitually start when making love to you?*
- *How long does he/she spend on you?*
- *Which parts of your body make you feel sexy when they are touched? List them in order of preference, and think not just about the obvious areas, such as your genitals, breasts, and nipples, but also about the less obvious regions. These include, for example, your scalp, hair, armpits, torso, waist, legs, ankles, and feet.*

The Waist
The waist is not often thought of as an erogenous zone, but there are many ways of touching it to create arousing feelings. It can be stroked, licked, squeezed, and kissed for erotic effect, and some people like to have their navels touched and licked.

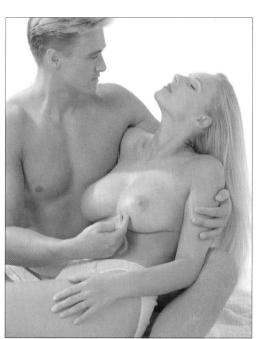

Breasts
A woman's breasts and nipples are obvious erogenous zones, but those of most men will also respond arousingly to manual and oral stimulation.

Suitable touch
Vary the nature of the touch you use so that it suits the area of your partner's body, and to match his or her preferences.

GAINING INFORMATION

Although it has become easier to talk about sex today, there is one aspect of lovemaking about which young people know even less now than they did 40 years ago. Thanks to the contraceptive pill making intercourse "safe" (that is, not resulting in unwanted pregnancy), couples in new relationships tend to begin having intercourse without getting to know each other physically beforehand. The result: they miss out on gaining valuable, basic sexual information. The only good result of living in a world with HIV *(see page 154)* is that we have begun to learn methods of lovemaking other than intercourse.

BREAKING STEREOTYPES

Many men incorrectly assume that women like their genitals approached quickly and directly at the beginning of lovemaking. This is because many men choose this approach for themselves. Similarly, many women assume that men find it hard to be passive and dislike women taking the initiative in lovemaking. Yet there are men who long for the woman to make at least some of the moves first, some of the time. By learning about each other's preferences, you and your partner can avoid thinking in terms of these old stereotypes.

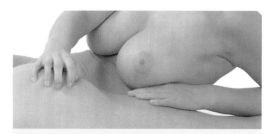

TOUCH INTENSITY QUESTIONNAIRE

This questionnaire, like the Sexual Body Questionnaire on page 41, is one that you can work through together with your partner. It is intended to give each of you an insight into how the other likes to be touched during foreplay and intercourse.
- Do you like:
  rough touch
  soft touch
  firm touch
  light touch
- Do you prefer touch to be:
  fast
  slow
- In lovemaking, is it more exciting if:
  you take the initiative
  your lover takes the initiative
  everything happens spontaneously

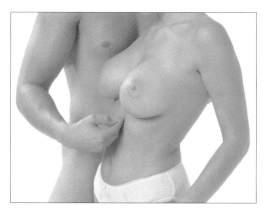

The Chest
Although not as sensitive as the breasts, the rest of the chest will respond pleasurably to sensual touch. Try light, teasing strokes and slow, lingering caresses.

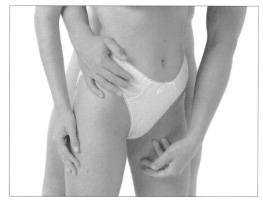

The Thighs
The most sensitive parts of the thighs are the insides, and the closer the touch is to the groin, the more exquisite and arousing will be the sensations touching engenders.

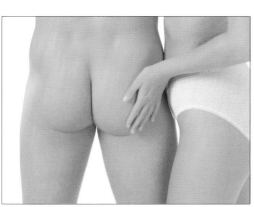

The Buttocks

There are numerous ways of touching the buttocks to create arousing feelings, ranging from featherlight caresses to squeezing and even spanking.

The Backs of the Legs

The fleshy back parts of the legs are generally more sensitive to touch than the fronts, and the hollows at the backs of the knees are especially so.

MUTUAL PLEASURE

In finding out about each other's responses to touch, you are also learning how to use it to give each other sensual pleasure.

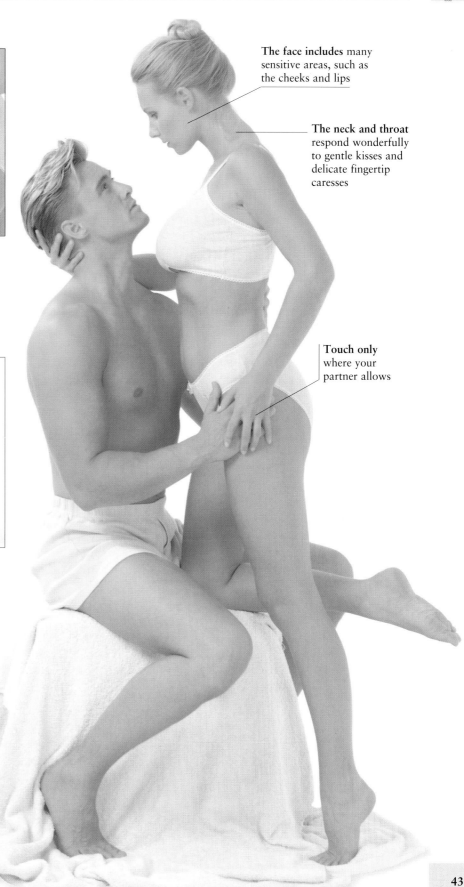

The face includes many sensitive areas, such as the cheeks and lips

The neck and throat respond wonderfully to gentle kisses and delicate fingertip caresses

Touch only where your partner allows

A Man's Sensuality

To help you get a clear picture of your partner's erogenous zones, begin by taking a look at the order of preference with which he rated the parts of his body in our Sexual Body Questionnaire *(see page 41)*. Then carry out the Sensitivity Test, which will help you to visualize the pattern of his erotic responses.

Warm touch
Just as you do before giving a massage, ensure that your hands are comfortably warm before you begin your exploration of your partner's skin.

With your partner lying unclothed, carry out the Sensitivity Test by exploring and stroking the preferred areas of his body with your fingertips. As you do so, ask your partner to rate your strokes on a scale of plus three to minus three. For example, if something feels wonderful, he might rate this as plus three; if there is little sensation, as either plus one or zero; or if it feels unpleasant or painful, he could use the minus ratings. In this way you can build up a detailed mental image of what feels good to him and what does not.

TEACHING INCREASED RESPONSE

It is possible to build up erotic sensation with rhythmic stimulation once your partner feels you have got the touch right, but this is just a fact-finding mission: there is no orgasmic end in mind. Your job is to gain information, and his is to offer it. Together, you are working out the best possible combination of your ability to touch and his ability to appreciate it.

THE PENIS AND TESTICLES

The American sex researchers Masters and Johnson found that, instead of remaining at one expanded size, there are degrees of expansion for the penis during sexual arousal. If penile stimulation is prolonged, apparently well-established erections continue to expand. Although this expansion was demonstrated using oral or manual methods of stimulation, Masters and Johnson hypothesize that there is every reason to think the same expansion would continue during prolonged intercourse.

The testicles begin to expand in diameter late in the arousal phase. The only times when testicular expansion was not demonstrated in the Masters and Johnson survey was when men ejaculated very rapidly after onset of stimulation. If sexual excitement is kept high for a long time without

Lie unclothed
on a bed or
comfortable sofa

the release of ejaculation, then most men experience a severe ache in the testicles. This can be quickly relieved by ejaculation.

THE NIPPLES

In 1979, Masters and Johnson published a valuable study of homosexual behaviour. One of its findings was that homosexual men usually pay much more attention to their partners' nipples at the beginning of foreplay than do heterosexuals, and they stimulate them both manually and orally.

Heterosexual couples can learn from this. Part of what makes any area of the body feel good when touched is a sense of comfort and an acceptance of that touch. Even if a man's nipples have never possessed much sensation before, it may be possible, through some good experience and practice, for him to respond erotically.

STROKING ACTION
When you are carrying out the Sensitivity Test, use light but firm pressure and make short, circular strokes with your forefinger and middle finger.

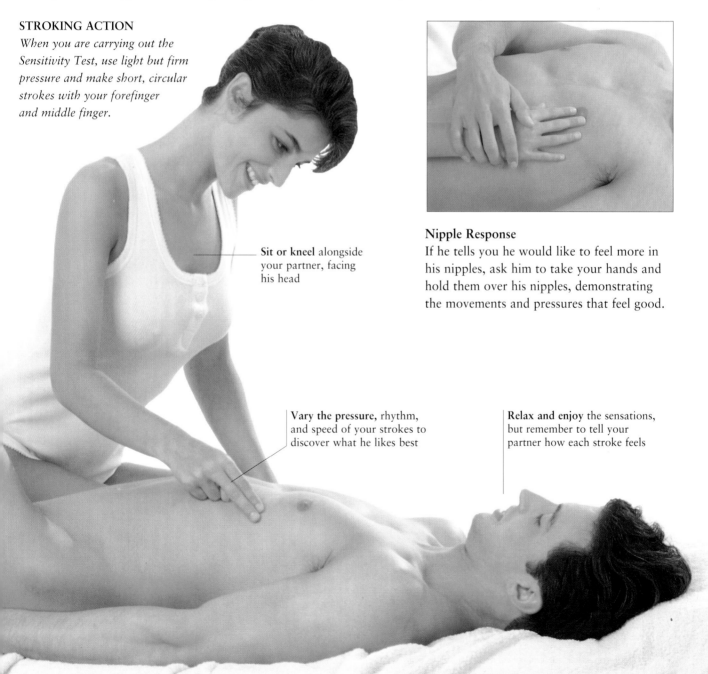

Nipple Response
If he tells you he would like to feel more in his nipples, ask him to take your hands and hold them over his nipples, demonstrating the movements and pressures that feel good.

Sit or kneel alongside your partner, facing his head

Vary the pressure, rhythm, and speed of your strokes to discover what he likes best

Relax and enjoy the sensations, but remember to tell your partner how each stroke feels

MALE SEXUAL ANATOMY

The principle male sex organs are the penis and the testicles, with the penis being the more important as far as foreplay and intercourse are concerned. However, the common belief that the size of the erect penis is a guide to a man's virility, reproductive ability, or performance as a lover is totally mistaken. What matters is the skill with which he makes love.

Penis size depends almost entirely on race and build. Smaller races such as the Thai possess smaller penises (but these are in proportion to their overall height and weight), and stocky men are more likely to have big penises than slight, wiry men. As with faces, every penis is unique in shape and appearance. None looks exactly like another, but there are, of course, certain shared characteristics.

A penis may be either uncircumcised or circumcised. An uncircumcised penis is one where the foreskin is retained; the foreskin encloses the glans (head) of the penis when it is flaccid and retracts back behind it when the penis is erect *(see page 48)*. The foreskin can be short, barely covering the glans of the penis, or long and projecting beyond it. A circumcised penis is one that, for health or religious reasons, has had the foreskin either partially or totally removed.

The foreskin and the skin covering the shaft of the penis are likely to contain hair follicles and often small spots. These spots are not

SELF-KNOWLEDGE
Knowing about your own sexual anatomy will help you to recognize any physical problems that may arise.

the result of ill health; they are simply oily sebaceous glands and are quite normal. Penile colouring depends on overall skin colour, but it changes when the penis becomes erect, and it deepens with age. If there is any unusual change in its colour, and the foreskin is ballooning and creating great discomfort, the reason might be a penile infection, which can often be caused by too tight a foreskin. Circumcision would overcome this difficulty.

After a circumcision, there might be some scar tissue on the penile shaft just behind the glans, depending on how skilfully the operation was carried out. If it was carried out for purely medical reasons, such as an infection or adhesions between the foreskin and the penile shaft (making it difficult or impossible to draw back the foreskin), the scarring may be greater.

PENILE CURVATURE
Many penises curve slightly or hang naturally to one side or the other. This is normal and healthy. But if a penis is unnaturally bent, its owner might be suffering from Peyronie's disease (the formation of dense fibrous tissue within the penis) and he should seek medical advice.

In mature men, the opening on the head of the penis is normally a small slit, but the shape can vary. What is important is that it should be dry: a discharge usually indicates an infection, and medical attention is required. Inflammation may be the result of poor hygiene, but if it is accompanied by a discharge, seek medical advice.

THE TESTICLES
These consist of two clearly separate testes (felt as small, rounded balls) hanging within the scrotum. It is normal for one of them to hang lower than the other. If there appears to be only one testis within your scrotum, you may have an undescended testicle. In this event, seek medical advice.

HYGIENE AND HEALTH

Uncircumcised men should clean beneath the foreskin regularly. If they don't, then when the foreskin is slid back there will be a white, smelly, cheesy substance beneath it. This is penile smegma, an accumulation of skin oils and dead skin cells which is the direct result of inadequate hygiene.

The penis and scrotum naturally possess a distinctive smell, which intensifies if the owner is aroused and secretes (normally) a pre-ejaculatory fluid. The pioneering American sex researcher, Alfred Kinsey, found that 78 per cent of male subjects were aware of doing this. In the majority, this fluid consisted of only a drop or two, but in nearly 20 per cent of subjects there was enough to drip from the penis. One theory about this fluid is that it releases sexual pheromones (chemical attractants) that contribute to the female arousal.

It is useful for a man to know and be comfortable with the normal smell of his genitals and penile secretions, because then he will quickly notice any abnormal smell, which could signify ill health. Illnesses that can produce offensive-smelling discharges include non-specific urethritis (NSU), syphilis, gonorrhoea, and trichomoniasis. Other important signs of venereal infection are discomfort or pain when urinating, and itchiness, rashes, and sores. In addition, the foreskin, meatus, and anus can conceal herpes (which may also be the cause of a discharge) and genital warts *(see below)*.

Any man experiencing one or more of these symptoms should visit his doctor – or, better still, a specialist clinic – as soon as possible, and refrain from any sexual activity until the problem has been cured.

GENITAL WARTS

These are soft, cauliflower-shaped growths caused by the human papilloma virus (HPV), which can also cause cancers, including cervical cancer in women. Because this virus may be transmitted sexually, anyone who has them (whether male or female) should not have intercourse without using a condom *(see page 154)*.

CROSS-SECTION OF THE MALE SEX ORGANS

Sperm is produced in the testes and stored in the epididymis duct. *From there, it travels along the* vas deferens *to the seminal vesicles, where it is mixed with seminal fluid before ejaculation. At ejaculation, both seminal vesicles, the prostate gland, and urethra contract to expel semen through the tip of the penis.*

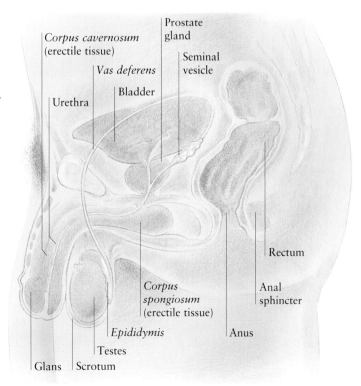

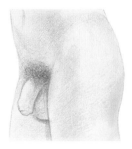

Uncircumcised penis

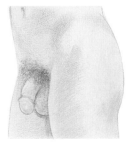

Circumcised penis

MALE SEXUAL RESPONSE

In general, men are more quickly and easily aroused than women, but after orgasm they usually have to wait much longer before they are ready and able to have intercourse again. The most obvious sign of male arousal is erection of the penis, but this is only one of a number of physical changes that occur.

Messages of sexual arousal from the brain or the spinal cord can travel to the genitals within ten to 30 seconds of stimulation. With men, the principal effect of this is erection of the penis, which is caused by the intricate network of vessels within its spongelike erectile tissues (see page 47) filling with blood.

In addition to penile erection, the testes are pulled up toward the body and the wall of the scrotum gets thicker and tighter. If stimulation is prolonged or intensified, the testes are pulled right up and increase in size. As sexual excitement increases, blood pressure rises, and heart rate and skin temperature increase. The pupils dilate, and the nipples may become erect.

Muscle tension in men also increases during arousal. Breathing becomes almost hyperventilation and many men experience a "sex flush", a kind of reddish rash under the skin of the head and chest. After orgasm, these changes disappear quite rapidly, and for a varying length of time (known as the *refractory period*), few men can be stimulated once more to climax.

ORGASM

Alfred Kinsey described the male orgasm as "an explosive discharge of neuromuscular tension" during which "the individual suddenly becomes tense, momentarily maintains a high level of tension, rises to a new peak of maximum tension – and then

MALE SEXUAL ANATOMY DURING AROUSAL

Erection occurs when the erectile tissues of the penis – the corpus cavernosum (of which there are two) and the corpus spongiosum *– become filled with blood. At the same time, the testes are drawn up closer to the body, the skin of the scrotum thickens, and the prostate gland enlarges. These changes are quickly reversed after orgasm.*

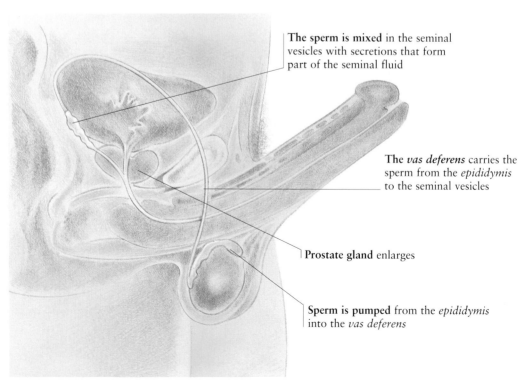

The sperm is mixed in the seminal vesicles with secretions that form part of the seminal fluid

The *vas deferens* carries the sperm from the *epididymis* to the seminal vesicles

Prostate gland enlarges

Sperm is pumped from the *epididymis* into the *vas deferens*

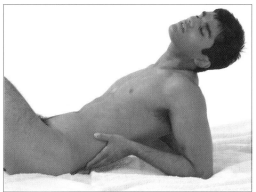

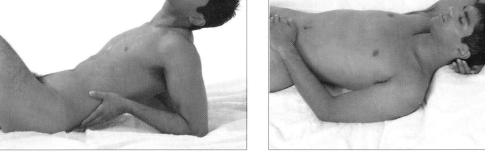

Sex Flush
During the most intense phase of sexual arousal, about 25 per cent of men show a reddening below the skin of the head and chest.

Muscle Tension and Heartbeat
During sexual arousal, the muscles become increasingly tense, the heart rate increases, and there is a slight rise in blood pressure. These changes intensify until after orgasm, when the body reverts to normal.

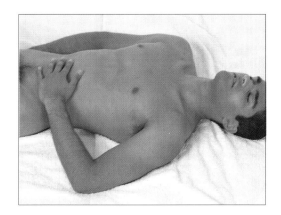

Nipple Erection
Up to 60 per cent of men experience nipple erection when they become sexually aroused, but the remaining 40 per cent or so show no visible signs of erection.

abruptly and instantaneously releases all tensions and plunges in a series of muscular spasms, or convulsions, through which he returns to a normal or even subnormal physiologic state."

Men recognize that orgasm is imminent when they reach what's known as the "point of no return" – a sense of inevitable ejaculation. The semen is pumped out through the urethra by short bursts of intense muscular contraction. Interestingly, the rhythmic muscular contractions of the penis during ejaculation occur at the same rate as do the contractions of the vagina during female climax (see page 57).

The amount of semen ejaculated varies considerably and can be anything between one and six millilitres in volume, that is, up to about a teaspoonful. If there is repeated ejaculation over a short period, the amount of semen produced each time gradually diminishes. On the other hand, if a long time has passed since the previous ejaculation, the amount produced is likely to be relatively large.

Orgasm can lead to an altered state of consciousness. This, in most men and women, means simply a sense of being "on a different level" of the brain, rather than of actually losing consciousness.

THE MALE RESPONSE CYCLE

In the latest definition of the sexual response cycle, its first three stages are desire, arousal, and orgasm. Desire is a hard-to-quantify emotion, which some say is an attitude of mind and others the product of hormone activity, and it often blends with the next stage, arousal. Some men become aroused with little or no physical stimulation but others may need a great deal. As stimulation continues, by hand or during the thrusting of intercourse, a man's arousal and excitement intensify and lead to orgasm and ejaculation. Excitement and erection then subside and he enters the *refractory phase,* in which his body slowly returns to normal. During this period, some men may be able to have another erection, but usually not another ejaculation.

MALE MULTIPLE ORGASMS

There are men who have demonstrated, under laboratory conditions, that they are capable of more than one orgasm in a session. Research by American sex researchers Hartman and Fithian indicates that multiple orgasm in men is not linked with ejaculation, and one conclusion is that men may be able to experience climaxes without ejaculation.

Hartman and Fithian have studied men who claim to climax repeatedly, although it is not clear that the reported orgasms are anything other than peaks of excitement and arousal. Sex researcher Alfred Kinsey has documented that boys who have not yet reached puberty, and therefore not developed the ability to ejaculate, were nevertheless capable of orgasm. Not only were they capable, but they were able to repeat the orgasm within a few minutes, and nearly a third of them were able to achieve five or more orgasms in rapid succession. But this ability soon disappears with the arrival of puberty, although some young men are able to get a second erection fairly soon after climax and begin again.

MUSCLE CONTROL

The men studied by Hartman and Fithian seem to have achieved multiple orgasms by tensing their thigh muscles and squeezing their pelvic floor or PC (pubococcygeal) muscles, thus blocking off their ejaculations by closing their urethral tubes with muscle action. This is like an internal version of the squeeze technique of ejaculation control *(see page 95)*. But because the male climax is so associated with ejaculation,

TRAINING FOR MULTIPLE ORGASM

Flexing the PC muscles
The first prerequisite is to develop your PC (pubococcygeal) muscles and inner groin muscles. To exercise them, try to wave your penis around by using these internal muscles only. You can also strengthen them by trying to lift a towel with your erect penis, and by trying to make your penis throb inside your partner. To gain real control of these muscles, you need to exercise them at least twice a day, and probably a lot more.

Testicle control
The testicles rise automatically before ejaculation; if your testicles don't elevate, you can't ejaculate. By learning how to raise them, you may be able to make ejaculation easier, and if you can lower them, you may be able to prevent ejaculation. Stand with your feet about 45 cm (18 in)

apart and pull your testicle muscles up toward your lower abdomen. Repeat as many times as you can, gradually increasing the number every day. If the testicles begin to hurt, stop, and do not continue until the next day.

Erection maintenance
Give yourself an erection and then continue it for as long as possible by both manual and emotional stimulation. Start by trying for a minute a day for the first week and build up from there.

Myotonic exercise
Climax is triggered by a kind of tension in the pelvic area called *myotonia*. To build up this myotonia, alternately flex and relax your legs and lower abdomen for as long as possible: five minutes is the aim, but if you get cramp, stop.

LABORATORY STUDIES

In their laboratory tests of men who claimed to be multiorgasmic, Hartman and Fithian wired their subjects up to instruments that measured such factors as breathing, heart rate, and muscle tension. The subjects then masturbated, observed by the researchers and monitored by the instruments.

In an account of one of these tests, Hartman and Fithian describe how, just before the man's first orgasm, his breathing quickened, his heart began beating much faster than before, and his pubo-coccygeal muscles squeezed firmly on the pressure transducer (detector) in his anus. After ejaculation, he continued masturbating and his breathing became deeper and slower, before quickening again as he ejaculated for a second time. This was repeated five more times, giving a total of seven distinct orgasms in ten minutes.

It is perhaps worth noting, however, that in the first ejaculation, a small amount of semen oozed rather than spurted from his penis, and only a few drops were produced on each of the subsequent ejaculations.

nobody knows, even in the laboratory, if these multiorgasmic males were actually climaxing or were simply experiencing peaks of excitement. Whatever it was that they were doing, however, they were clearly undergoing an intense and prolonged sexual experience.

GENITAL FITNESS
According to Nick Konnoff, who was a star subject of Hartman and Fithian's laboratory tests, there is a training routine to help you achieve the same response that their multiorgasmic males managed.

This routine consists of four sets of simple exercises *(see opposite)* that constitute a sort of fitness regime for the male genitalia. They also reproduce the physiological conditions of the sort of sexual arousal that lasts over a long period of time. You may find that you need more sex as a result of doing the exercises. You may also find that your climaxes, when they arrive, are experienced more powerfully.

MULTIPLE CLIMAX PRACTICE
Once you feel that you have achieved genital fitness, now is the time to put it all into practice. Equip yourself with whatever you need for your comfort and for your stimulation. Excite yourself slowly and erotically, building up to a high pitch over a long time, using the myotonic training exercise to heighten your sexual tension.

When you feel orgasm about to break, clench your PC muscles and, to be on the safe side, be prepared to pull down on your testicles by hand if the voluntary muscular control of the testicles feels as if it's not going to work. Don't be dismayed if the first few efforts fail and orgasm appears inevitable. Developing the degree of muscle control that is necessary often takes time.

WARNING
Just because a very small number of men can manage a form of multiple orgasm, even in the artificial conditions of being tested in a laboratory, that does not mean that all men can. But even if you are not able to become multiorgasmic, the exercises will increase your genital fitness and give you greater ejaculatory control.

In addition, if you start concentrating single-mindedly on ejaculation training when you are in a relationship, you can create the likelihood of the relationship, and the individual who is your partner, being overlooked by sexual ambition. At the end of the day, it is the quality of the lovemaking that is valuable, not just the physical sensation of orgasm.

A WOMAN'S SENSUALITY

An erogenous map of a woman's body would show that her sensual feeling is more diffused than that of a typical man. The peaks of her sexual sensation will correspond to those of the man, but her ears, neck, shoulders, hands, and toes are more likely to be erotically sensitive. Use the Sensitivity Test *(see page 44)* to form a mental picture of your female partner's erotic responses. Does it match your preconceptions?

To help your partner increase her response to sexual stimulation, build up a variety of sensation on the less obviously erotic places, such as the neck and the shoulders, and on the torso at the sides of the breast. By stimulating these areas with stroking, light scratching, gentle biting, and tongue bathing, and then proceeding, believe it or not, to the feet, you will induce a highly charged state of sexual desire in your partner's body. Then, and only then, you can touch her genitals to find out how much she feels and where.

THE BREASTS

In their 1979 study of homosexual sexual response, Masters and Johnson found that lesbian women, when making love, began by holding, kissing, and caressing each other's whole body for much longer than heterosexual couples do. When the lesbian couples finally turned to specific parts of the body, the breasts received much more attention, and for far longer, than was typical in heterosexual lovemaking.

The whole breast was caressed, both manually and orally, with special concentration on the nipples. Approximately equal amounts of time were taken on each breast, and sometimes as much as ten minutes was spent on breast caressing before turning to the genitals. The woman being stimulated always produced copious vaginal secretions at this time, and on two separate occasions one of the study subjects actually climaxed strongly during breast play alone, before her genitals had been touched.

Interestingly, the women in Masters and Johnson's study of heterosexual couples reported that their breasts were not a particularly erogenous zone to them. There are lessons to be learned from this, probably the most important being that even if heterosexual women don't experience much breast sensation, they have the potential for it. Experimenting with breast massage is one way of awakening a woman's erotic breast sensation.

THE CLITORIS

A man can probably maximize his partner's response to clitoral stimulation by following a similar procedure to that employed by the lesbian women in Masters and Johnson's studies. These women almost always caressed each other's labia, mons pubis, inner thighs, and vaginal entrance *before* touching the clitoris. And when clitoral stimulation had begun, even though the head of the clitoris may have been stroked initially, the focus of the stimulation usually became the clitoral shaft.

Neck and Shoulders
To begin exploring your partner's responses to stimulation, gently kiss her lips and then work your way slowly down her neck and across each of her shoulders.

The couples used two main sorts of sex play. The first was a "teasing cycle", in which one partner stimulated the other to the point of orgasm and then allowed her arousal to subside before stimulating her further. In the second, one partner stimulated the other with more continuity and increasing intensity until she climaxed. Lesbians rarely used their fingers to penetrate each other's vagina. This happened quite regularly among the heterosexual couples, however, but the women involved derived little pleasure from it.

The Torso
The sides of the torso can be surprisingly responsive to touch, especially to light, brushing, fingertip strokes and to licking and gentle nibbling.

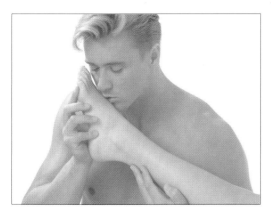

The Feet
Work on every part of her feet, from her ankles to the tips of her toes. Try sucking her toes and running the length of your forefinger through the gaps between them.

GENITAL STIMULATION
Leave her genitals until last. Your aim should be to find out more about her response to stimulation of her labia, vagina, and clitoris, and not, at this point, to try bringing her to orgasm.

Use one hand to caress her breasts

Kiss her lovingly while you caress her

FEMALE SEXUAL ANATOMY

Since the majority of women don't get the same "locker-room" opportunities as men to observe each other's genitals, it can be very much harder for them to understand their own anatomy and be comfortable with it. Because of this, many women may find the following information about the female genitalia especially important.

The external female genitalia are referred to collectively as the vulva. This consists of the outer labia (vaginal lips); the inner labia; the clitoris, which is usually covered by the mons pubis or pubic mound (the fleshy pad above the genitals, clothed in pubic hair); and the entrance to the vagina. Inside this entrance, near the top, is the urinary opening.

The outer and inner labia vary greatly in size. Some women have small, fleshy outer labia and long, hanging inner labia. Others possess highly developed outer labia, and very small inner labia that look like a fringe around the vaginal entrance. And there are dozens of styles in between.

The outer lips are often hairy on the outside but, when pulled open, show a paler shade on the inside. The inner lips may also be a paler colour on the inside than on the outside. The colours deepen with age.

It is normal for one labium to hang lower than the other and for one side of the clitoral hood to fall lower than the other. It is also normal for

SELF-KNOWLEDGE
Learning about your sexual anatomy will help you to understand your responses to sexual stimulation.

some women to possess extremely hairy genitals and for others to have virtually no pubic hair. There is great variation in genital appearance from one woman to another.

THE CLITORIS

Situated at the top of the labia, the clitoris may protrude like a tiny penis, may look like a tiny button, or may only come into sight when the pubic mound above it is pulled back. Kinsey reports that it averages something over 2.5 cm (1 in) in length, but since most of it is embedded in the soft tissue that surrounds it, only the glans (head) shows. As with male genital proportions, clitoral size also probably depends on body size and build.

The shaft of the clitoris is usually covered, and this has given rise to the idea of the "hooded" clitoris. There is a false idea that if the clitoris is so hidden, the woman can experience no sensation. Cosmetic surgeons still, therefore, make money through giving women unnecessary operations to get rid of such a hood.

In fact, only a tiny number of women need such an operation. They are the women whose skin is attached with some adhesion to the shaft of the clitoris, so that when their clitoris erects during sexual excitement it is prevented from moving freely and so the woman experiences pain. (The male equivalent would be the man who can't retract his foreskin.) But these women are exceedingly rare. The main reason for a woman's lack of sexual response is usually that her clitoris doesn't get sufficient stimulation, because intercourse alone doesn't provide enough.

HYGIENE AND HEALTH

It is normal for the vaginal entrance to be slightly moist, and it is usual for women who are menstruating to experience regular vaginal secretions (of a greater or lesser degree) during their monthly menstrual cycles. A teenage girl who is experiencing regular secretion is not sick, nor does she have a sexual disease. Her body is telling her that it is functioning properly. It is unfortunately necessary to write this since clinics still report mothers dragging in their frightened teenagers, complaining that such secretions indicate that they must have had sex.

One of the worst activities of the health products industry has been to teach women that their genitals smell bad and so they should use vaginal deodorants. These deodorants may actually be harmful for women, if they rid the genitals of their natural secretions.

There is a slightly sweet smell to healthy female genitals, and this odour has a distinctly aphrodisiac effect on many men (Napoleon, for example, allegedly sent messages to his lover, Josephine, telling her not to wash before his arrival home). If there is a truly unpleasant smell, however,

it signals a vaginal discharge resulting from a sexual infection or disease and needing medical attention. An abnormal vaginal discharge is one that flows continuously and is usually (but not always) foul-smelling. If you are worried by such a discharge, seek medical advice, preferably from the venereal department of your nearest large teaching hospital.

Diseases that can cause discharge are *Gardnerella vaginalis*, trichomoniasis, non-specific urethritis (NSU), gonorrhoea, and genital warts *(see page 47)*. Diseases that produce sores or lumps include syphilis, thrush, herpes, and genital warts.

Always seek prompt medical advice if you discover any of these symptoms, and if you find any tiny open cuts or sores on the moist inner parts of your genitals. These are often caused by thrush, which can be cleared up by topical creams, but any suspicious sores should always be given medical attention.

CROSS-SECTION OF THE FEMALE SEX ORGANS

The vagina extends up and back from the vulva, and it expands and lengthens during sexual arousal (see page 56). Many women have a small, extra-sensitive area, known as the G-spot, on the front wall of the vagina, typically half to two-thirds of the way in. When stimulated in the right way, it can trigger orgasm.

THE VULVA

Gently opening the labia majora *(outer vaginal lips) reveals the* labia minora *(inner lips), the urethral opening, and the entrance to the vagina.*

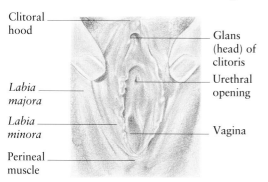

Clitoral hood

Glans (head) of clitoris

Urethral opening

Labia majora

Labia minora

Vagina

Perineal muscle

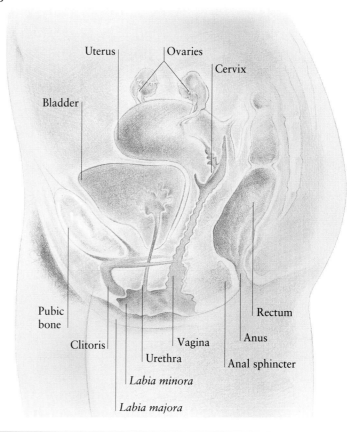

Uterus

Ovaries

Cervix

Bladder

Pubic bone

Clitoris

Vagina

Urethra

Labia minora

Labia majora

Rectum

Anus

Anal sphincter

FEMALE SEXUAL RESPONSE

Although a woman's genitals are mostly hidden within her body, their external parts – principally the clitoris, the inner and outer labia, and the opening to the vagina – are extremely sensitive to touch. Despite this sensitivity, women are generally not as quickly aroused as men, but after orgasm it takes longer for their arousal to subside.

The first sign of female arousal is vaginal lubrication. The vagina lengthens and distends, and the vaginal walls change to a darker colour because of engorgement with blood. This engorgement, which in men is responsible for filling and elevating the penis *(see page 48)*, in women fills and elevates the labia and the clitoral shaft.

The breasts swell, the nipples become erect, and the uterus and cervix begin to move upward. Heart rate and blood pressure increase, while a sex flush – a reddish, rash-like skin coloration – appears on some parts of the body. As excitement grows, many muscles become tense. Women have a variety of bodily reactions to extreme sexual arousal, including jerking the limbs and body and even trembling violently all over. Some women start thrusting their genitals spontaneously against their partners. During extreme excitement, the outer third of the vagina (the orgasmic platform) closes a little due to the swelling caused by the increased blood supply. The engorged inner labia change colour dramatically to a brighter or deeper red.

When the woman has entered the *plateau phase* of arousal, prior to orgasm, her uterus also engorges and continues to increase in size, at the same time rising farther in the pelvis. This creates the condition known as *tenting*, which is caused when this elevation lifts the cervix and leaves a hollow space at the far end of the vagina which isn't there at other times. Also, during this phase, the walls of the vagina exude a secretion.

Once this level of increased sexual tension has been reached, the clitoris seems to disappear – it retracts into the swollen pubis – and the tissues around the nipples swell with fluid so that the areolae enlarge. This enlargement has the effect of making the nipple erection seem to disappear. Heart rate and blood pressure continue to increase and breathing often becomes rapid and shallow.

THE FEMALE RESPONSE CYCLE

A woman's sexual response cycle, like that of a man *(see page 49)*, begins with desire. Arousal and excitement are the next stages, and while some women get very rapidly aroused and are ready for orgasm almost immediately, others take far longer: some women need up to 45 minutes of stimulation before orgasm becomes possible.

The arousal phase is followed by orgasm, in which orgasmic contractions occur in a similar way to those of the man. The majority of women then experience a loss of sexual and muscular tension after orgasm as their bodies return to their normal physiological condition.

But there is a major difference here between male and female sexual response in that a minority of women, unlike men, can remain highly aroused and capable of further orgasms. Dr Helen Singer Kaplan, of Chicago, has noted that each of these phases – desire, arousal, and orgasm – can be experienced separately as well as in a sequence.

Sex Flush
In most women, a sex flush appears during the excitement phase of the response cycle, intensifies with increase arousal, and is at its most intense at orgasm.

Muscular Tension
General tension of the muscles and limbs increases with increasing arousal, and it often culminates, at orgasm, in powerful, involuntary muscular spasms.

ORGASM
Climax begins with muscular contractions, originating in the orgasmic platform, which contracts rhythmically as sexual tension is released. Masters and Johnson found that these orgasmic contractions usually occurred from three to 15 times and at 0.8-second intervals, decreasing in frequency and intensity after the first few. This pattern of contractions is the same as that of the penis during a man's ejaculation. Sometimes, a woman's uterus and anus also contract simultaneously and powerfully during orgasm.

At the moment of orgasm, breathing is at least three times as fast as it would be normally, the heartbeat more than double its usual rate, and the blood pressure is increased by one-third. Most of the body muscles are tense.

After orgasm comes the *resolution phase*. During this phase, in some women the body returns to its previously unstimulated state, with the clitoris returning to its normal size and position, the vagina returning to its normal size, and the uterus and cervix dropping back to their normal position. In other women, however, the body merely drops back into the excitement stage before going on to further orgasms (provided that stimulation continues).

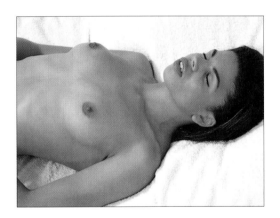

Nipple Erection
Nipple erection begins in the excitement phase and peaks at orgasm, but may be hidden by enlargement of the breasts and areolae during intense excitement.

STATUS ORGASMUS
There is also a particular orgasmic response, noted by Masters and Johnson, which they call *status orgasmus*. In this, a few women are able to have a rapidly recurrent set of orgasms with no intermittent resting phase (see page 58).

Women who experience this orgasmic response may be able to identify different peaks of excitement, or they may simply feel that they are going through an intensely long and drawn-out climax, with no identifiable separate peaks.

FEMALE MULTIPLE ORGASMS

In terms of the ability to have orgasms, women are in some respects the luckier of the two sexes. Although it is a minority of females who are capable of more than one climax, there are still considerably more of them than able men. There can be no promises, however: advice on these pages will not, unfortunately, automatically equip you to become multiorgasmic.

Multiple orgasm can be experienced in a number of different ways, but it usually consists of a series of separate orgasms occurring within a short time, sometimes with only a few seconds between them, sometimes with longer intervals. Some women experience multiple orgasm as a series of gentle peaks of excitment that feel connected, while others simply have one strong climax after another, each one seeming to run into the next.

STIMULATION
To be able to achieve multiple orgasm, of course, a woman needs continuing stimulation after her initial climax. Her partner must be able to control his ejaculation so that he can keep thrusting, or else provide her with manual stimulation after he

himself has climaxed and withdrawn. The chances of having sequential or multiple orgasms are also greatly increased if the woman is given a high level of sexual stimulation before intercourse begins. If the man is loving and patient, and willing to delay intercourse, he can use his fingers, hands, and mouth to bring his partner almost to the point of orgasm before he penetrates her.

ORGASMIC CAPABILITY
Not all women are capable of multiple orgasms, and not all women want them. Many women find satisfaction from one good orgasm, and there are others whose bodies feel too sensitive for continuing stimulation after one orgasm.

No one yet knows why some women, but not others, should be able to have multiple orgasms, but one theory has it that the ability is due to high levels of free-ranging testosterone (a hormone) within the body. As far as we know, our hormone levels are either random or may be inherited in the same way as other physical characteristics. A woman's overall state of health is also known to affect her hormone balance, however, as do medications such as the contraceptive pill.

TRAINING FOR MULTIPLE ORGASM

Increase arousal
Useful techniques for increasing your level of sexual arousal include enjoying a dramatic sexual fantasy, watching a sexy movie, and delaying orgasm. Instead of going for orgasm at the first possible opportunity, wait. Put it off, again and again, until you reach an extreme pitch of arousal (some women find this easier and less tiring to do if they use a vibrator instead of their fingers).

Continue stimulation
When you reach climax, continue with the stimulation. You may find that your orgasm goes on much longer than you might have expected.

Think positively
If you accept, on first climax, that you're finished for the day, then you're likely to be just that. Try keeping your mind full of erotic thoughts.

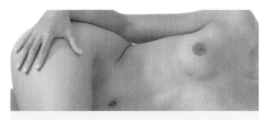

LEVELS OF ECSTASY

Many ancient teachings on sex describe the ecstasy of female orgasm. The Taoist belief is that there are nine levels of female arousal, but Western women, apparently, rarely receive the stimulation that is needed to get beyond Level Four. In Yogic tradition, the man rides a "Wave of Ecstasy" produced by his partner. He delays his orgasm while she has four (the "Four Joys"), each lifting the couple to a higher plane of ecstasy. After her fourth orgasm, they climax together.

More-easily aroused women can usually experience multiple orgasm during intercourse. But there is a group of women who discover, often in their late 20s or early 30s, that they can learn how to have more than one climax when stimulating themselves or perhaps while someone else is masturbating them.

Women are considered to be at a sexual peak in their early 30s so maybe, again, this is reflecting high testosterone levels. But it can also reflect a better knowledge of one's own sexual response, a willingness to persist in something new, and a greater patience and confidence.

Encouragingly, studies have shown that not only does women's overall capacity for orgasm (whether through intercourse or masturbation) increase with age, but that women in their 30s are much more likely than younger women to be capable of having multiple orgasms.

MULTIPLE ORGASM PRACTICE

If you have not experienced multiple orgasms but want to discover if you are capable of being multiorgasmic, you might like to try a simple training programme *(see opposite)* while masturbating. Success cannot be guaranteed, alas, but you can enjoy trying.

This programme is based on three basic principles: a high level of arousal is more likely to result in a multiple orgasm than is a low level; multiple orgasm requires continuing stimulation after the initial climax; and developing a positive attitude, combined with a belief in your own abilities, helps to overcome any subconscious barriers to multiple orgasms – give yourself permission to enjoy them.

Telling each other sexual fantasies will increase your arousal

AROUSAL
A high level of sexual arousal before your initial climax, and continuing stimulation after it, can help you to have multiple orgasms.

SENSUAL MASSAGE

  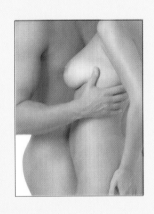

One of the best things about massage, apart
from the pleasure it gives, is its versatility.
For example, you can use it to soothe tired
muscles and to relieve the stresses of everyday
life. You can also give your partner a massage
as a prelude to lovemaking, or as an exciting
and very sensual alternative to intercourse.

SENSUAL BODY MASSAGE

Most of us believe that feeling sensual is allowable only within the framework of lovemaking, preferably with a committed partner. To expound the notion that there is a wealth of wonderful sensation at our fingertips, which we are capable of giving to (and receiving from) practically anyone, feels almost immoral. Yet there is nothing wrong in giving pleasure to others or to ourselves. We do it already in many other ways, for instance by giving food and friendship.

Accepting that we all deserve such pleasure, and that there is nothing wrong or abnormal about it, opens us up to great delights. The starting point for this comes in the shape of whole-body sensual massage. You don't have to do this with a committed partner for it to be sensational, but of course it feels especially good when you offer your tantalizing touch to the one you love.

On the following pages you will find the massage strokes that make up a whole-body massage. Before we discuss them, spare a little time to consider some important details. These are details that make the difference between a matter-of-fact present of touch and a mysterious, overwhelming, spiritual gift. That's a strong promise, but massage can offer stimulation for the brain as well as for the body.

PATTERNS
As you get to know which strokes you feel most comfortable with giving, you will understand that it makes sense to carry out strokes in certain patterns. For example, working your way up one side of the body and then down the other is a pattern. And alternating grand, sweeping strokes with little, detailed strokes is another pattern. Remember to include as much of the body as possible so that no part feels left out.

TIMING
Massage, especially when you're not used to doing it, is tiring, so don't overdo it on the first occasions. I always feel so overwhelmed by a good back massage that I don't instantly long for my front to get attention, but many people feel cheated if the front is ignored. If both front and back massage is required, cut down on the number of strokes for each so that what you do deliver is done with freshness and energy.

Don't expect to use every single one of the strokes described on the following pages. To conserve your energy, try a few different ones on every occasion; this will also help you to learn which are the most effective. If asking for feedback proves brutally intrusive, remember to check with your partner afterward for details of how he or she enjoyed the massage.

A SENSUAL EXPERIENCE
One of the keys to making a massage truly heavenly is to feel it yourself as a sensual experience. Close your eyes, feel the sensation on your hands, and alter your touch so that it pleases you as well as your partner.

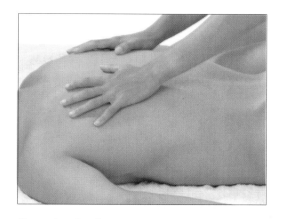

Sweeping Strokes
When you are massaging relatively large areas of the body, such as the back, use long, sensuous, sweeping strokes and try to keep the sensations your partner feels as smooth and continuous as possible.

TEN GOLDEN RULES

- Respect your partner's requests
- Honour any agreement you make in advance of the session, for example that intercourse is not on the agenda
- Keep your massage movements slow
- Be aware of the sensations you receive when giving a massage
- Try to tune in to your partner's reaction to your massage gift
- Never foist a massage on someone who says he or she does not want it
- Make a point of gently asking your partner for feedback
- When it's your turn to be massaged, remember to give your partner plenty of tactful feedback
- Ensure that you have privacy
- Make sure that the room, your hands, and the massage oil are warm

AGREEMENT
Before you begin, you should both agree exactly what is going to happen during the session, and change your plan only by mutual consent.

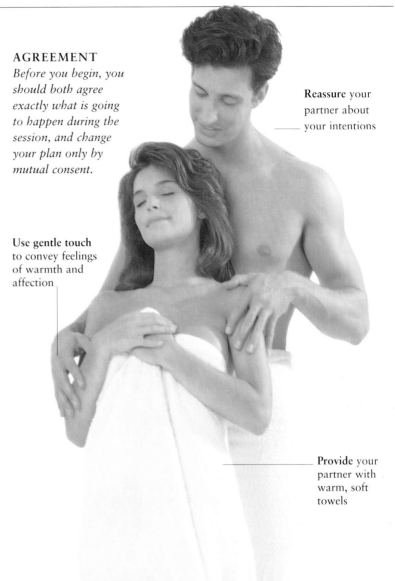

Reassure your partner about your intentions

Use gentle touch to convey feelings of warmth and affection

Provide your partner with warm, soft towels

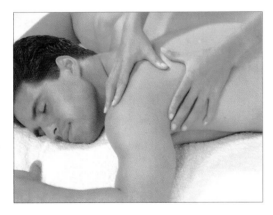

Detailed Strokes
The strokes you use on the smaller, more complicated parts of the body, such as the shoulders, hands, and feet, should be short but decisive. Avoid massaging areas where the bone is close to the skin.

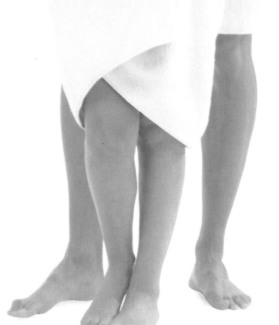

SETTING THE SCENE

For a sensual massage to be truly successful, the surroundings in which it is given are as important as the technique and skill of the masseur. The room should be attractive, comfortable, and carefully lit, and should provide adequate privacy to ensure that you are not going to be interrupted.

COMFORT
A massage should be unhurried and carried out in warm, comfortable surroundings.

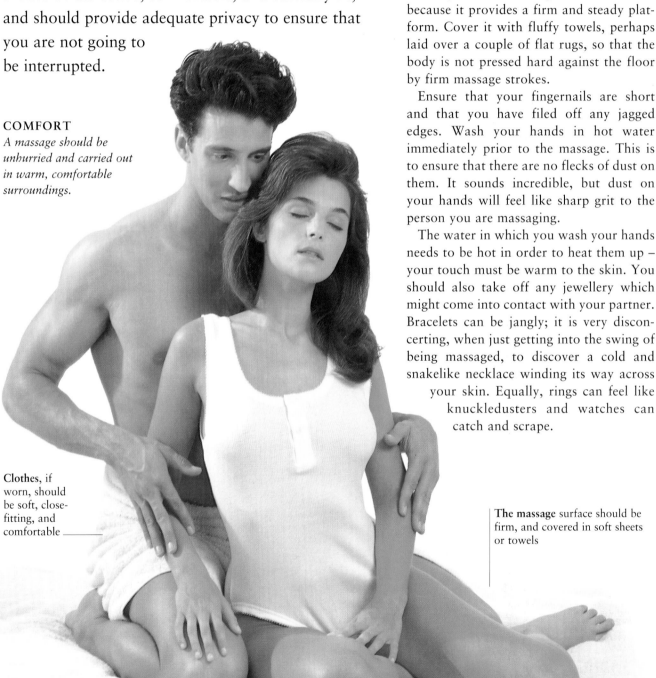

Clothes, if worn, should be soft, close-fitting, and comfortable

Make sure that the room is warm, and there are no draughts. Cold air makes the skin tense, and you experience touch as pain instead of as pleasure. The best place to carry out the massage is on the floor, because it provides a firm and steady platform. Cover it with fluffy towels, perhaps laid over a couple of flat rugs, so that the body is not pressed hard against the floor by firm massage strokes.

Ensure that your fingernails are short and that you have filed off any jagged edges. Wash your hands in hot water immediately prior to the massage. This is to ensure that there are no flecks of dust on them. It sounds incredible, but dust on your hands will feel like sharp grit to the person you are massaging.

The water in which you wash your hands needs to be hot in order to heat them up – your touch must be warm to the skin. You should also take off any jewellery which might come into contact with your partner. Bracelets can be jangly; it is very disconcerting, when just getting into the swing of being massaged, to discover a cold and snakelike necklace winding its way across your skin. Equally, rings can feel like knuckledusters and watches can catch and scrape.

The massage surface should be firm, and covered in soft sheets or towels

Warm up the massage oil in advance by putting the oil bottle in a bowl of hot water. When you are applying it, do not on any account drop it directly onto your partner's body. This will be experienced as an extreme shock. It makes the body tense involuntarily and altogether negates the sensual relaxation at which you are aiming. Instead, pour a little oil into one hand then rub your hands together to give each palm a liberal coating.

CLOTHING

Massages are best received in the nude: even a pair of briefs constitutes a barrier to complete enjoyment. To the masseur, underwear is irritating; to the massagee, any stroke that has to avoid the clothed area feels incomplete. But if you, as masseur, feel uncomfortable in the nude, stretchy clothes such as close-fitting briefs and a close-fitting T-shirt are best, because they won't swing free and trail ticklingly over the massagee.

SOUND

Some people like soft and tasteful music playing in the background during a massage session. But if you don't have a machine that will repeat the tape or disc, or play several tapes or discs one after the other, the player should be positioned near you so that you can easily put on something new. If music is part of the spell you are creating, it can be distracting if it suddenly stops. It may be better to have no music at all. Loud music or heavy rock is also not advisable because it will detract from the sensual atmosphere.

SCENT

The smell of incense is an erotic addition to the ambience of the massage scene. You could use burning joss sticks or warm sweet-smelling oil in a candle-fired burner, heating it until its fragrant vapour rises into the air and pervades the room.

The massage oil itself should also smell exotic. Baby oils and oils that smell "clinical" simply are not sensual. I've always enjoyed using suntan oil of the expensive variety because I love the evocative memories of hot sun and sand. Many herbalists and health stores stock oils suitable for massage, and if you want a stronger smell, you can always add a perfume to these oils.

SIGHT

A scruffy room littered with junk is not going to have the same visual impact on the would-be sensualist as is the room with exotic colours and low lighting. Clean towels, sheets, and coverings are essential. And if oil spills are likely, do make sure that the massage surface is protected by covering it with something washable, such as a towel. If there is a spill, wash the towel as soon after the massage as possible to avoid staining.

ESSENTIAL OILS
Blend your own massage oil by adding a few drops of an essential oil, for example rose, camomile, or rosemary, to a base such as almond oil.

AMBIENCE
Candles provide gentle, romantic lighting, and you can use an essential oil burner to create soft fragrances.

BACK MASSAGE

Many of these strokes can be used on the front of the body (*see page 72*) as well as on the back, but the back is the easiest part of the anatomy to begin with. It offers you a relatively large area of skin on which to work, and because it is less sensitive than the front of the body and can take more pressure, it is a good part of the body on which to discover how to adjust the pressure of your strokes.

Pressure is the secret of turning a routine massage into a sensual experience. A strong massage feels thorough and "medical", a lighter one pleasurable and sensual, and a fingertip massage arousing and erotic. Timing is also important: if you give someone a fingertip massage without preceding it with a firmer one, your touch can be felt as irritating or even tickling. The skin needs to be prepared for its

Circling
This is the first and most basic stroke, and it can also be used as a link between other strokes. Place both hands, palms downward, on the shoulders and move them firmly in opposing circles. Work out and away from the spine, progressing down the back and over the buttocks. Then work back up to the shoulders and repeat twice.

Lean gently forward onto your hands when you want to increase the pressure of the massage

Tell your partner if you want the pressure or speed of the strokes increased or decreased

Synchronize the circling movements of both hands

arousal, which may be why, when making love, time spent cuddling, stroking, rubbing bodies together, and sliding around each other is such an important precursor to more intimate foreplay.

Feedback from your partner will tell you which of your strokes feel good and which are less successful. Creating a mental "relief map" of your partner's erogenous zones *(see page 44)* can help you turn your massage into a truly skilful as well as sensual experience.

For a back massage, your partner lies face down. You kneel or sit alongside, and work up from the buttocks to the shoulders. Begin by coating your partner's back with warm massage oil, using sweeping, flowing strokes and spreading it generously over his or her skin.

When you start on the massage itself, don't forget the golden rule: take it slowly. Being lingered over is far more sensual than being rushed at like an old washboard, so take your time. And, as a general principle, if either of you feels that things have gone ahead too far, too fast, go back a stage so that you both feel secure again.

Hairline Circling
After circling up the back, massage from the tops of the arms across the shoulders to the neck and let your thumbs circle into the hairline.

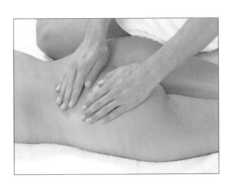

Cross-Currents
This is a variation of circling. Use the palms of your hands, moving them close together in opposing circles, and work over the fleshy areas of the back and the buttocks.

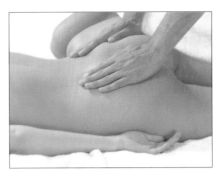

The Glide
Place both hands flat on the buttocks, then lean forward and let your weight push your hands up your partner's body. Repeat once.

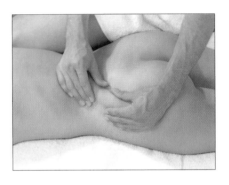

Kneading
Kneading is good for the hips, the buttocks, and the fleshy areas of the back. Using the thumbs and forefingers of both hands, rhythmically squeeze and release the skin.

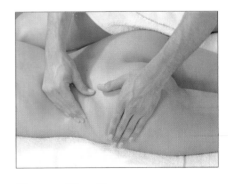

Alternate Kneading
In this variation of the basic kneading stroke, you gently squeeze your partner's flesh with each hand in turn instead of using both hands simultaneously.

Keep your legs flat on the ground or bed

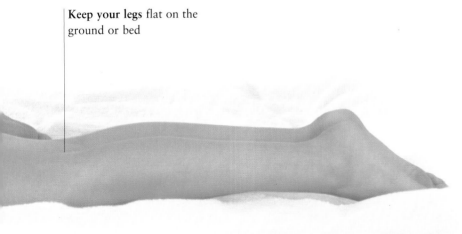

Easing the Lower Spine

The base of the spine takes the constant pressure of keeping the body upright all day. This soothing lower spine massage is intended to relieve some of the tension caused by that pressure. To begin the massage, kneel astride your partner and place a hand on either side of the spine, just below the waist, with your fingers pointing sideways.

Lean forward and use the weight of your upper body to create the pressure of your massage

Relax your upper-body muscles so that the effect of the massage is not diminished by your muscular tension

Give your partner's skin a liberal coating of oil so that your hands glide smoothly over it

Lower Spine Massage

Lean heavily on your hands and let your weight force them slowly apart, so that they slip down the sides of the body to the ground or bed. Just before your hands reach the ground or bed, repeat the stroke, starting a little nearer the base of the spine. Repeat as many times as your partner wants.

TOPPING UP

To apply more oil, keep the back of one hand resting on your partner's skin, cup it, and pour a little oil into it.

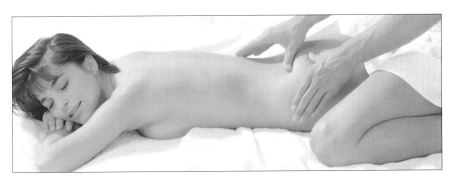

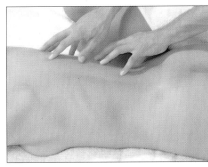

Thumbing
Using both thumbs, make short, rapid, alternate strokes on the lower back. You can either move your thumbs in circular strokes or simply push them upward. Beginning on your partner's buttocks and gradually moving up to the waist, work your way up one side of the back and then up the other.

Clawing
With only your fingertips resting on the skin, pull down firmly hand over hand along one side of the body and then the other.

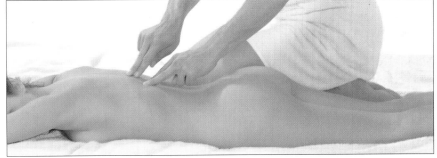

Stop-start Clawing
Work your middle and forefingers along the "grooves" on each side of the spine. Pull one hand down a few inches, then as you take it away, press down with the other, in the opposite groove, starting just below where the first hand finished. Continue all the way down the spine, and repeat two more times.

THE CATERPILLAR

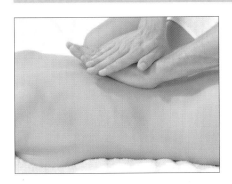

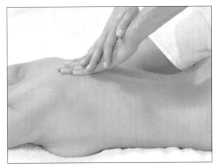

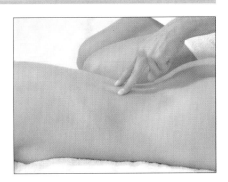

1 Sit at your partner's side and place your left hand on the base of the spine, pointing to the head. ·Place your right hand flat on top of your left.

2 Slowly glide forward and back, forward on the palm and back on the fingers, pushing down with the right hand and working your way caterpillar-like up the spine.

3 At the top, take your right hand away. Draw the first two fingers of your left hand slowly down each side of the spine, pressing hard. Repeat the strokes two more times.

69

Body Rocking
Kneel at the right-hand side of your partner, reach across with your left hand, and slip your fingers under his or her body. Pull up to lift the body

CAUTION: Body Rocking and the Hip Lift can be difficult on a heavy person. With a heavy partner, you will put less strain on your back if you kneel on one knee and one foot, but if your partner is too large for you to lift safely, avoid these movements altogether.

Make sure your fingers are thoroughly coated with massage oil so that they slip easily under your partner's body

slightly, then release it. Slip your right hand under the other side and repeat the stroke. Pull rhythmically, on left then right, to set the body into a rocking pattern.

The Hip Lift
Glide your hands down your partner's body from the shoulders to the buttocks, then slip your hands under the hips and draw them up the underside of the body. This will lift the body slightly. Repeat once.

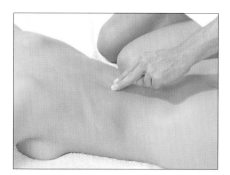

Spinal Tap
Press your thumbs into the indentations on either side of your partner's spine, and draw them slowly down until you reach the base. Repeat, varying the pressure.

The Thumb Slide
In this reverse version of the spinal tap, push your thumbs firmly up on either side of the spine, drawing them from the base to the hairline. Repeat, again varying the pressure.

One Hand Only
Press on the spine just below the neck with your forefinger and middle finger, then slowly pull them down the spine, keeping the pressure even. Repeat.

The Raised Shoulderblade

This is quite a difficult stroke to do, so don't panic if you find it hard. The first stage is to fold one of your partner's arms across the back, then slip your arm under the forearm until the elbow is resting in the crook of your arm. Now lever up your arm slightly, and you will see your partner's shoulderblade lift.

Thumb Pressure

The second stage of the raised shoulderblade stroke is to press your thumb into the space below the blade, then draw it out to the armpit. Do this three or four times, then repeat on the other side.

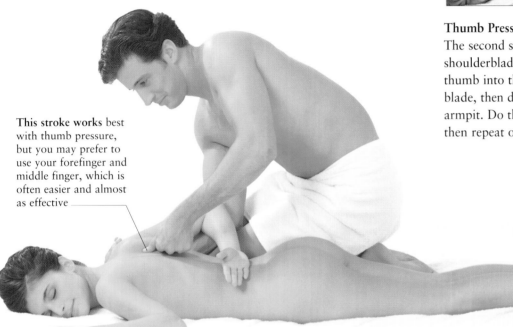

This stroke works best with thumb pressure, but you may prefer to use your forefinger and middle finger, which is often easier and almost as effective

FINISHING OFF

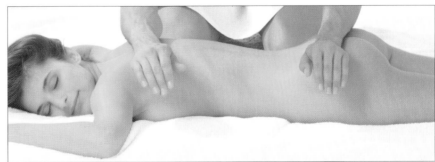

1 Kneeling at your partner's side, place the backs of your forearms close together across the centre of his or her body. Then very slowly spread your arms apart and turn them slightly inward.

2 By the time your arms have reached the neck and buttocks respectively, the fronts of your forearms should be in contact with your partner's body. When your arms meet the neck and buttocks, *lift them off and repeat the stroke immediately. On the third repetition, slow the movement right down and, when you reach the end, lift your arms off as gently as possible and sit quietly.*

FRONT MASSAGE

In addition to the strokes shown here, many of those used in back massage (*see pages 66–71*) can also be used in front massage. If you are following up a back massage with a front massage, help your partner turn over slowly. Rolling over, rather than sitting up suddenly, is the gentlest method. If there is likely to be a pause between massages, have warm towels ready with which to cover your partner so that his or her body doesn't lose heat.

Begin by coating your partner with massage oil. If your partner is male and has a hairy chest, apply extra oil to it so that your fingers don't catch. If your partner is female, remember to include her breasts in the massage (*see page 76*).

In back massage, circling is the basic stroke and the one that is used to link other strokes. In front massage, the slide takes its place and is the best stroke with which to begin the massage. When using the slide, kneel at your partner's head and place your hands, palms down, on the chest, with the heels of your hands next to the armpits. Then lean forward and slide your hands down over your partner's body.

Next, give your partner a shoulder lift and head lift, and caress his or her head. Then work on the upper chest, using the fairy ring strokes on the upper chest and cupping strokes on the breasts.

The Slide
Lean forward and let your weight carry your hands down the body until you can reach no farther; repeat two or three times. If your partner is female, reduce the pressure when your fingers begin to slip over her breasts.

Kneel with one knee at either side of your partner's head

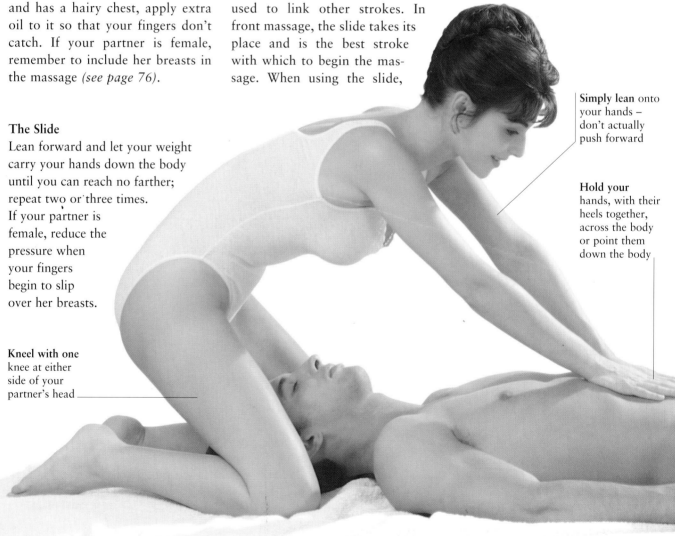

Simply lean onto your hands – don't actually push forward

Hold your hands, with their heels together, across the body or point them down the body

The Shoulder Lift
Slip your hands underneath your partner's shoulders, then firmly draw them up and out, lifting the shoulders slightly as you do so.

The Head Lift
A variation on the shoulder lift is to pull your hands along the underside of the head, with your fingers against the back of the neck.

Caressing the Head
Keeping your partner's head supported, repeatedly draw each hand in turn from the nape of the neck to the crown.

Fairy Rings
Using the fingertips of both hands and starting at the collar bones, make tiny circles over the whole of the upper chest except the breasts.

Cupping the Breasts
Using cupped hands, gently rotate the breasts as fully as possible, moving them clockwise, anticlockwise, and in opposite directions.

CONSTANT TOUCH

An important rule of massage is that when you are giving someone full-body strokes, your contact should be continuous. Never break your touch: you should always try to have at least one hand in contact with your partner's skin. This rule applies whether you are massaging the front or the back, and also when you are pouring out more oil during a massage *(see page 68).*

Circling the Belly

It is sensible to leave the belly massage strokes until last, because by this stage in the session your partner's body will have got used to being touched and ticklishness is less likely. Should ticklishness be a problem, however, you can usually overcome it by using a firm touch. Massage in a clockwise direction (the direction in which the colon runs), and use the palm of one hand to make full circles along the outer rim of the belly.

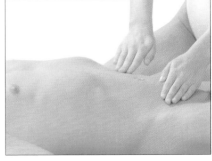

Using both Hands

Vary the belly circling strokes by using your other hand as well. Make semicircles with it from hip to hip, moving in the same direction as the first hand and lifting off every time that hand comes around.

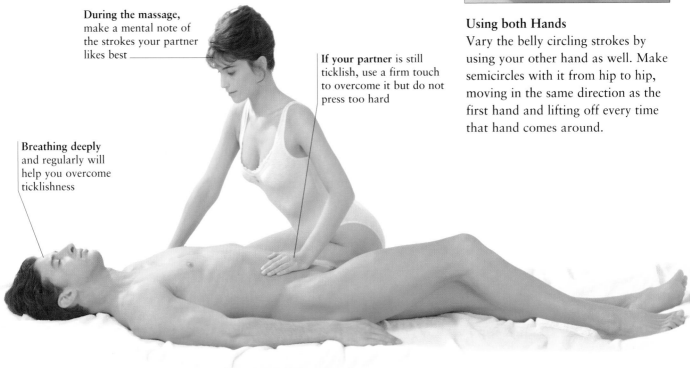

During the massage, make a mental note of the strokes your partner likes best

If your partner is still ticklish, use a firm touch to overcome it but do not press too hard

Breathing deeply and regularly will help you overcome ticklishness

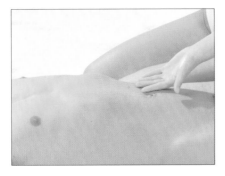

Hand Twisting

Continue your clockwise circles with one hand, only this time twist the hand itself for part of its run so that you are then massaging with the back of the hand.

Kneading

This is done on the front of the body in exactly the same way as it is on the back (see page 67), focusing on the fleshy sides of the body around the waist and the hips. As before, you can use both hands either simultaneously or alternately, and once you've covered all the suitably fleshy areas, vary the sensation by doing deep circling with the tips of all the fingers.

The Abdominal Slide
In this stroke, you slide your hands firmly but gently up your partner's abdomen from groin to ribs. Before you start, straddle yourself comfortably across your partner's thighs. Place both palms on your partner's

lower abdomen, with your fingers pointing toward the head. Then push your hands (not by leaning on them, because your weight would be too much) slowly up the abdomen until your fingertips meet the ribcage. Repeat as desired.

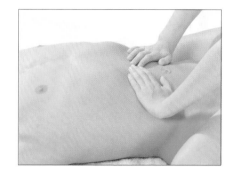

The Abdominal Twist
To vary the slide, twist your hands so that their heels face outward and the fingertips meet at your partner's middle. Gently sweep these apart below the ribcage so that your fingertips trace the bottom ribs.

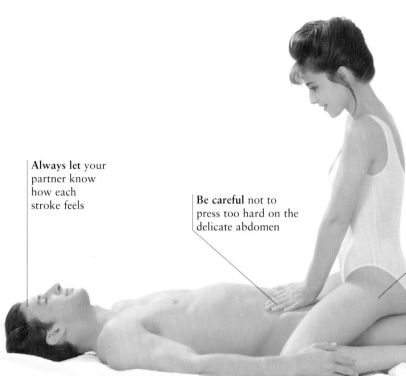

Always let your partner know how each stroke feels

Be careful not to press too hard on the delicate abdomen

The straddling position helps you to synchronize your hand movements and keep your strokes symmetrical

THE SECOND SPINAL TAP

1 This is an excellent finishing move, but you must be careful with it if your partner is heavy (see page 70). Slip your hands underneath each side of your partner's waist and bring your fingertips to

either side of the spine. Keeping the backs of your hands against the floor, press up with your fingertips firmly enough to lift your partner a fraction. Hold for a count of twenty and then let down slowly.

2 Put your hands beneath your partner and lace your fingers tightly together under the spine. Then pull up and toward you, so that your partner is lifted slightly and then settles gently back.

BREAST MASSAGE

When you are giving your female partner a body massage, don't be afraid to include her breasts in the routine – if you omit them from it, she may be left feeling that the massage is unfinished. This simple but very sensual four-step breast massage routine was devised by the noted Californian masseur, Ray Stubbs.

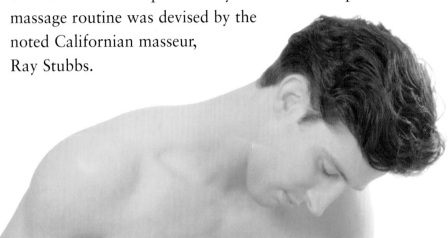

PERFORMING THE MASSAGE

1 Slide the flat of your right hand diagonally across her right breast, moving toward her left shoulder. Then slide your left hand across her left breast in the same manner. Repeat these two strokes alternately, about six times each.

INTIMATE POSTURE
When giving a breast massage, either kneel at your partner's side or, to make the experience even more intimate, support her head on your thigh.

To make the massage as sensual as possible, coat her breasts and your hands with massage oil before you begin, and use light, delicate strokes

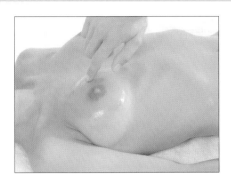 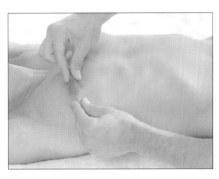 

2 Using a well-oiled fingertip and the lightest possible touch, trace out a spiral on one of your partner's breasts. Start on the outer side and spiral in until you reach the nipple, then repeat the stroke on the other breast.

3 Gently squeeze a little skin at each side of the nipple, and very lightly slide outward as though your fingers were moving along the spokes of a wheel to its rim. Repeat this stroke on all of the "spokes" of each nipple.

4 Squeeze the nipple gently between well-oiled forefinger and thumb, sliding them up and off it. For extra effect, you can use both hands alternately so that the action, and the sensations, are continuous. Repeat on the other nipple.

" Heather's Experience

I reached the age of 45 without ever feeling much sensation in my breasts. It seemed that even the most skilful attention from a lover's fingertips, lips, or tongue was not enough to trigger any truly erotic responses from my nipples and breasts.

But then I got into a relationship with a new lover, a marvellous man who, as I was to discover, was gifted with magic fingertips. One memorable evening, we were just lazing around in bed, not making love but touching each other sensuously. He

simply circled and circled my breasts with his fingertips, stroking them and my nipples every which way.

Almost immediately they came alive, and felt like they were independent beings with an intense erotic life of their own. Every ripple I felt running through my breasts caused a corresponding ripple in my vagina. In the end, I pleaded with him to have sex and he wouldn't. He just went on and on stroking my breasts until I was gasping with excitement. I've never felt so aroused. "

Let your limbs relax, and luxuriate in the sensuous pleasure of the massage

ARM MASSAGE

When I was given my first-ever massage, by an extremely skilled practitioner, he covered my arms and my hands as well as my back. Although I experienced less sensation in my arms than in my back, it still felt utterly right that they should be included, and the hand massage was wonderful. What was less than sensational for me might, of course, be spectacular for someone else, because we possess widely differing patterns of sensitivity in our arms. The insides of the arms and the insides of the wrists are, however, excellent candidates for tactile attention. Here are my suggestions for making the most of whatever sensations we find.

There are two schools of thought about the direction in which an arm massage ought to go. People who learn "lymphatic" massage, which aims to improve the circulation, work up the arm from wrist to shoulder. Those whose thoughts are directed less toward health and more toward sensuality practise kneading, stroking, and pulling down the arm, from shoulder to wrist. I have included strokes from both regimens, and I leave it up to you to decide which suit you and your partner best. I've omitted the more vigorous of the usual arm

The Beginning
This couldn't be easier: it consists simply of holding hands. Peacefully holding hands is a marvellous act of friendship, and is undoubtedly a good way to get your partner in a terrifically receptive mood. It is also a jumping-off point for the rest of the massage.

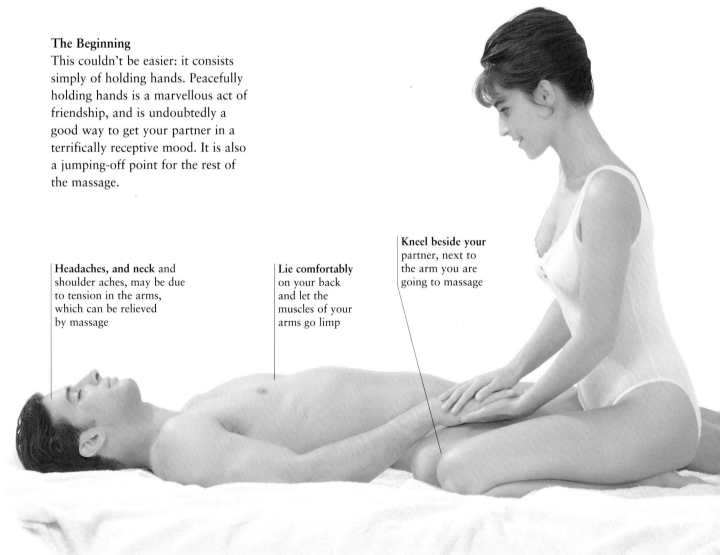

Headaches, and neck and shoulder aches, may be due to tension in the arms, which can be relieved by massage

Lie comfortably on your back and let the muscles of your arms go limp

Kneel beside your partner, next to the arm you are going to massage

massage strokes on the grounds that they aren't sexy enough for a sensual massage.

MASSAGE SEQUENCE

After oiling the arms, massage each one in turn, giving one arm the complete treatment before starting on the other. Press gently if the arm is thin, more firmly if it is fleshy, but avoid pressing on any bones (such as at the elbow or wrist) because that can be painful. Before beginning work on your partner's other arm, you may like to make the massage feel more complete by following it with a hand massage.

I describe a full hand massage on pages 82–83. You can use an abbreviated version of this routine to make the arm massage more complete, and a full version of it if you simply want to carry out a hand massage on its own.

One of the most striking parts of my own first massage was how I felt flooded with friendship and love when my teacher worked on my hands. I was amazed that such simple touch could evoke such strong emotion. In fact, I was so knocked out by it, I became convinced that if everyone in the world had a compulsory hand massage every day of their lives, there would be no wars and no violence. This is an eccentric viewpoint, of course, but one that would be fascinating to try and prove.

OILING AND SPOILING

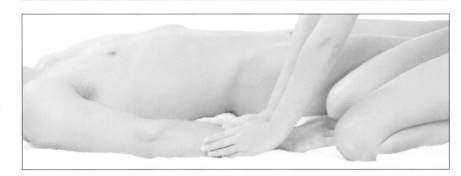

1 When you coat the arms in oil, slide both hands up them, side by side and with palms down. Work on each arm in turn, starting at the wrists and ending at the shoulders, and then working down again on the insides of the arms. The upward and downward strokes should not be separate but should blend together into one long, continuous movement.

2 Glide one hand smoothly up to the shoulder, the other to the armpit, then slide them down again.

Stroking
Use your fingertips to stroke your way down your partner's arm, pressing firmly and making short, overlapping strokes. These strokes should each be about 10 cm (4 in) long, and by overlapping them you make the sensation continuous. Work your way around and down the arm, and repeat once or twice.

Arm Kneading
Tuck your partner's hand into your armpit so that the arm stays more or less upright, and hold the upper part of this arm with your thumbs on the top. Circle your thumbs in opposite directions, working from armpit to elbow. Then lower the arm and continue kneading down to the wrist. Repeat each stroke twice.

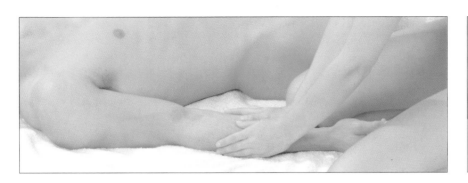

Draining

This stroke was designed to help improve the circulation in the arm. Begin by holding the arm with both hands at the wrist and thumbs on the inside of the arm. Pressing firmly with both thumbs, slowly slide them up to the elbow. Now bring your thumbs back down the arm to the wrist by drawing your hands, held flat, lightly along the sides of the arms. Repeat.

Twisting

Hold the wrists with your hands pointing in opposite directions. Then, twisting your hands in opposite directions, corkscrew your way up and down the arm, "stepping" over the elbow as you go. You will find that your corkscrewing comes to a natural halt on the upper arm, so take this as the cue to work your way back down to the wrists. Repeat twice.

Pulling

Holding the arm at the wrist, lift it straight up into the air, then pull it briefly and gently so that it stretches. Then let it relax, but without putting it down again. Repeat this light pull twice more.

Kneel rather than sit at your partner's side, so that you can pull the arm comfortably

THE ARMPIT STRETCH

1 *This is an excellent stroke on which to end. Position your partner's arm on the ground, stretched above the head so that the armpit is exposed. Place your hands, palms down and fingertips touching, on the armpit. With firm pressure, begin separating your hands so that the lower slips along the side of the body and the upper glides out along the arm. Lead with the heels of your hands.*

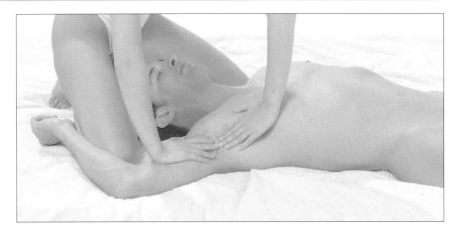

2 *Once they are clear of the armpit, twist your hands so that the fingers turn outward and the upper hand grasps the arm. Your lower hand should curve in so that it fits closely to your partner's torso. Increase the pressure, and continue slipping your hands sideways until your upper hand has reached the wrist and your lower hand is somewhere in the region of the hips.*

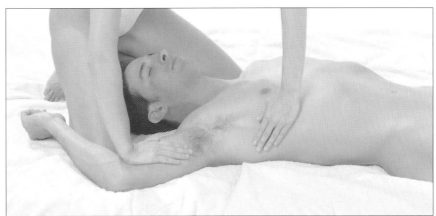

3 *Stop for a moment, holding on more tightly, and stretch your partner's arm and hip in opposite directions. Hold them stretched for a full second and then let go. Bring your hands rapidly down again to the armpit and repeat the stroke, but on ending it a second time, gently replace your partner's hand by his or her side.*

HAND MASSAGE

The hands are equipped with thousands of nerve endings in every square inch of skin. These nerve endings make the hands and fingers very sensitive indeed to stimuli such as touch, pressure, and temperature. Anyone who has ever cut a finger, or more especially a fingertip, will be able to testify to the acute pain the hands can feel; what I hope to bring you in touch with on these pages is the acute pleasure that can also be gained through the hands, by means of massage.

There are many similarities between hand massage and foot massage, but while you are giving hand massage you are also massaging your own hand. This is, of course, true of any type of manual massage: your hand receives touch as it gives it. But there's one aspect of hand massage that is like no other – it's called friendship. Hand on hand feels friendly.

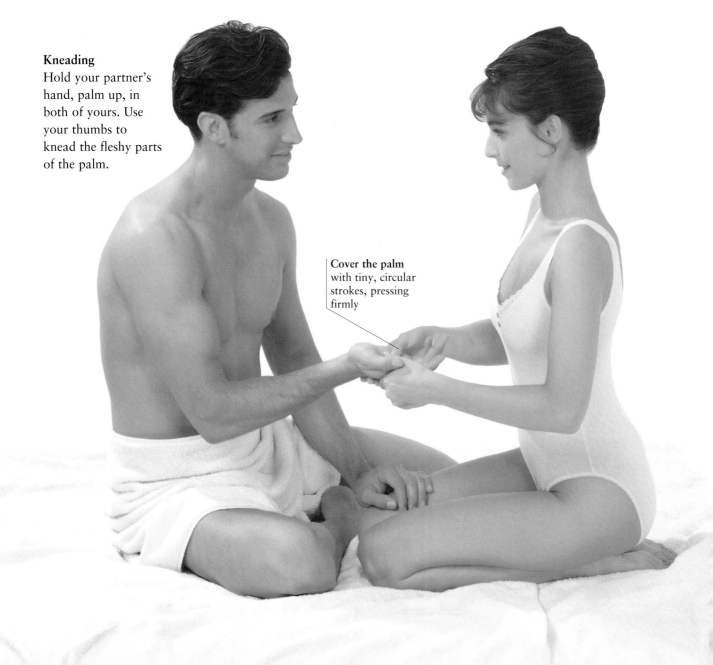

Kneading
Hold your partner's hand, palm up, in both of yours. Use your thumbs to knead the fleshy parts of the palm.

Cover the palm
with tiny, circular strokes, pressing firmly

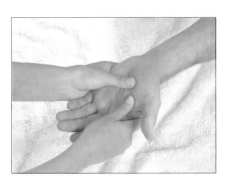

Palm and Thumb Massage
Use your thumb to massage the fleshy areas of your partner's palm and the base of the thumb. Then rotate each segment of the thumb between your thumb and forefinger.

Finger Manipulation
Taking your partner's thumb and each finger in turn, pull your thumb and index finger up the sides in short, corkscrewing strokes. On reaching the tip, work down again.

Knuckling the Palm
Press your knuckles into the palm of your partner's hand just below the fingers. Then scrape your knuckles from side to side, working your way toward the wrist.

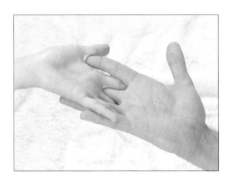

Finger Lacing
Lace your fingers through your partner's, palms up. Press against the back of your partner's hand so that the palm is flexed upward. Flex, then relax, three times.

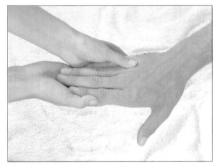

In the Groove
Starting at the wrist and finishing at the fingers, run your thumbpad down each of the grooves between the tendons on the back of your partner's hand.

Circling the Backs
Holding your partner's hand at each side, use both thumbs to circle all over the back of the hand, including the wrist. Massage with a firm but gentle pressure.

Circling the Wrist
Encircle your partner's wrist with thumb and forefinger, then lightly twist these several times from side to side around the wrist.

Stroking the Wrist
Draw the flats of your fingernails slowly from the base of your partner's palm up to the top of the wrist, then back down again.

Finishing Off
Hold your partner's hand between both of yours. Breathe deeply and imagine that your hands are sending energy into your partner.

LEG MASSAGE

Completing a task is as important as beginning it, and how you complete something often reflects your personality. If you're an impatient character, you might skimp the ending, to get the job over and done with quickly. But if you're a thoughtful personality, you might make the ending as lingering and as tactile as you did the start, and this is the approach to adopt for the leg massage, the final stage of a full-body massage. Here are the massage strokes for the backs of the legs; those for the fronts are on pages 86-87.

If you miss out massaging your partner's legs during your whole-body session, it will make the entire session less than satisfactory. Worse than that, your partner might wonder what it is that is so unattractive about their legs that you chose to ignore them. And instead of ending up feeling relaxed, sensual, even – if you're very lucky – ecstatic, your partner might instead feel let down, which would be a pity after all the hard work on your part.

When you massage the backs of your partner's legs, he or she should lie face down. Using a similar stroke to the one with which you oiled the arms *(see page 79)*, begin by massaging oil into the backs of the legs, one leg at a time.

Move forward on your knees as your hands work up the leg toward the buttocks

Make your strokes lighter as they pass over the back of the knee

Oiling and Spoiling
Starting at the ankle, work up to the buttocks and then down again. Place both hands on the ankle, one above the other with fingertips pointing in opposite directions, and slide them up the leg, spreading the oil up to the top of the thigh.

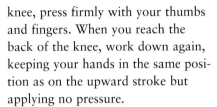

Draining

Place your hands, one above the other, around the ankle, with the thumbs uppermost and pointing in opposite directions. As you slide your hands up to the back of the knee, press firmly with your thumbs and fingers. When you reach the back of the knee, work down again, keeping your hands in the same position as on the upward stroke but applying no pressure.

Kneading

Use the kneading stroke here that was used earlier for the hips (see page 67). Work down from the thighs, kneading only the fleshy areas; omit the backs of the knees.

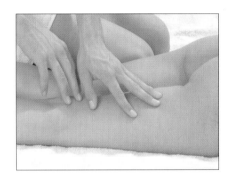

Deep-pressure Circling

Pressing the palms of your hands on the back of the leg, rotate the skin and the flesh below it in small circles. Do this on the fleshy areas only, and do not press too hard.

Hand over Hand

Starting at the thigh, draw one hand down 10 cm (4 in), then repeat with the other hand. In this manner, cover the whole of the back of each leg, working downward only.

Deep Finger Pressure

This is basically the same as the hand-over-hand stroke but, instead of using all of your hand, simply press firmly with your fingertips. Again, work downward only.

Finishing Off

Return to the oiling and spoiling stroke we began with, but make it very gentle. Repeat three times, and on the last returning strokes, slow right down and swivel your hands at the ankle so that one cups the back of the foot and the other the front. Then, exceedingly slowly, slip your hands away from the toes.

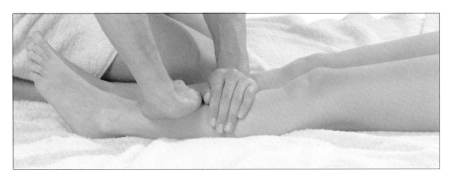

Oiling and Spoiling
Using a similar stroke to the one with which you oiled the arms *(see page 79)*, work the oil into the fronts of your partner's legs. Sweep your hands, palms down, fingers pointing in opposite directions and one hand placed above the other, up the front of each leg. Reduce the pressure when you pass over the kneecap, and continue up the thigh to the abdomen.

Kneecapping
This is much gentler than it sounds. Intertwine your fingers at the back of the knee, and then lightly circle the edge of the kneecap with the tips of your thumbs.

Return Strokes
When you bring your hands down again during oiling, separate them to each side of the leg and sweep them smoothly down in one long, sensuous, uninterrupted move.

Repeat the return strokes until the front of the leg has been fully covered with oil

Under Friction
Instead of circling the kneecap with your thumbs, place them both just below it, press them in, and slide them rhythmically together and apart like opposing pistons.

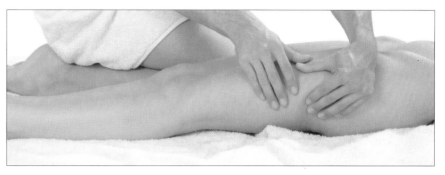

Kneading
Concentrating on the thigh only, knead the area with both hands, as you did when kneading the hips *(see page 67)* and the backs of the legs. Give each handful of flesh a gentle twisting motion as you squeeze. When you get used to the kneading action, you will be able to squeeze the flesh so that it appears to travel from one hand to the other with a short, wavelike motion.

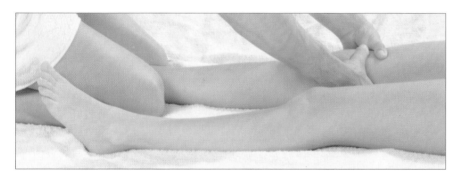

Draining
The fronts of the thighs are possibly the areas where the draining stroke is at its most effective. Use the same stroke as for the backs of the thighs *(see page 85)* and don't be afraid to use firm pressure here. I don't advocate using the draining stroke below the knees because it can feel downright uncomfortable. Also remember not to put any pressure on the kneecaps.

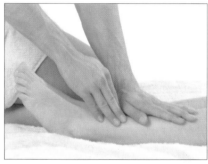

Hand over Hand
Use the same technique as for the backs of the legs *(see page 85)*. With a light touch, begin by being quick and brisk and then make it slow and sensuous.

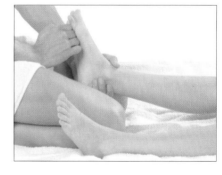

Finishing Off
When massaging your partner's legs, end with a hand-over-hand stroke at the foot. You might then try a foot massage *(see page 34)*.

INTIMATE MASSAGE

Giving an intimate massage is a gentle but
very effective way to masturbate your partner.
Use it as a sensational finale to a sensual
massage, as a highly arousing form of foreplay,
or simply for the pleasure it provides – you will
enjoy giving it almost as much as your partner
will enjoy receiving it.

EROTICISM

What makes an erotic moment? Is it an unexpected move or proposition? Is it the forbidden? Can any touch be thought erotic? Or does it have to be made with a specific intent? Perhaps each person has his or her own definition of what is erotic, and that definition is unique to that individual. An experience, thought, feeling, or suggestion that is incredibly arousing to one man or woman may do absolutely nothing for another.

But there's a difference between eroticism, lust, and even passion. If boy meets girl, and they look into each other's eyes and suffer the *coup de foudre* of instant attraction, even if they hurl themselves into the bedroom and feel quite savage with desire, it is not necessarily an erotic situation.

The very breath of eroticism contains leisureliness. It involves thought, deliberation, losing yourself in a sensual landscape where (and I'm sorry to sound corny) it's the journey and not the arrival that counts.

It's where an unexpected proposition or move might well be erotic because it puts sensual ideas into your head. And yes, the forbidden may be part of eroticism, but it's not the whole. For when you have glimpsed the sexual idea that is indeed erotic, the manner in which this idea is then translated into real lovemaking nearly always falls short of the thought.

MASTURBATION AND EROTICISM

Think of the man or woman who masturbates to pornography. He or she may enjoy a rich fantasy life and have wonderfully powerful orgasms. But the situation can't be erotic because there is no element of the unknown, no other person to inject a special, unpredictable quality into the lovemaking, no uncertainty, and therefore no certainty either.

Without these things we miss out on a dimension that includes trust in the other, confidence about oneself, and a liberating, breathtaking sense of openness in which we feel we can do anything and it will all be wonderful.

MAKING MASSAGE SENSUAL

I've described many massage strokes in the preceding pages, and when you've tried them, you and your partner will know which of them feel truly sensual and which don't. To augment these sensual strokes, the following pages contain suggestions for a more specifically sexual massage.

EROTIC MASSAGE
This is a wonderful form of foreplay, and can provide the high levels of arousal that some women need to help them reach orgasm.

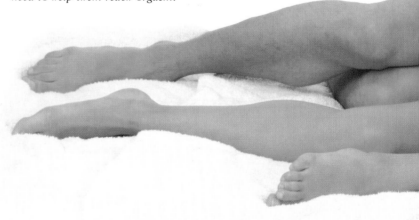

EROTIC RELATIONSHIPS

That's all very well, you might say, but how do you bring eroticism into an already established relationship, where you've been making love for some years? It's not surprising if you feel erotic with someone new – you've the novelty factor to help things along. What if, instead, you have the aging relationship factor to contend with?

Perhaps the key is being open to new ideas, because new ideas help us to develop mentally. On a profound level, this means you and your partner being truly open and honest about the state of your relationship, even if such honesty is painful and risky. On a physical level, being open to new ideas may mean having to accept that your lovemaking has become a dull routine, and that you need to experiment with something different.

CASE HISTORY
CLAUDIA AND EROTIC TOUCH

Some time after Claudia's long-term relationship broke up, she chanced to meet a man she had known years before. They had been good friends but never lovers, and she had never felt sexually attracted to him. The following evening, they went for a meal together, and afterwards he walked her from the restaurant to her car. As they walked, he slipped his arm around her and rested his hand on the side of her thigh. The effect was dramatic: it was as if, through that adventurous touch, she saw for the first time his daring, sensual, intensely physical side. She later told me that it had been one of the most exciting and erotic moments of her life.

Close bodily contact is an arousing accompaniment to an erotic massage

Use your hands as a means of transmitting your erotic feelings to your partner

Tell your partner which strokes you like best

FOR HER PLEASURE

This massage, and the following one for men *(see page 94),* is based on methods taught by Ray Stubbs, and also by graduates of the Institute for the Advanced Study of Human Sexuality in San Francisco. Interestingly, while all of the strokes for men came complete with title, none of the strokes for women were named so I have given them names myself. Remember – this massage should only be included after the rest of her body has been stroked and pleasured.

Gentle Hair Torture
Pull her pubic hair, gently and in small tufts. Using both hands at a time, work your way slowly from the top of her pubic hair and down each side of the labia.

Duck's Bill
Shape the fingers of one hand into a "duck's bill", hold them above her clitoris, and pour warmed massage oil over them so that it slowly seeps through and runs onto her genitals.

THE GENTLE HAIR TORTURE
The idea is not, of course, torture, but to cause exquisite pricking sensations that travel from the mons pubis straight to that delicate sex organ, the clitoris. Take a long time over this, to lay the foundation for much more intimate pleasuring.

DUCK'S BILL
This is experienced by the woman as a flooding sensation, full of warmth but slightly disturbing – which is as it should be. She should, of course, be lying on towels so that any spillage of oil falls into the towelling. Please ensure that the oil is warm, and do be careful to avoid getting any actually inside your partner's vagina, because it might prove difficult to disperse.

WIBBLING
As little children, many of us experiment with pulling the bottom lip of the mouth down and letting go. If you do this quickly and often, it makes a "wibble" sound. If you don't believe me, try it for yourself.

When you've got the hang of it, you will be able to try some "genital wibbling" on your partner. Start with one of the outer labia (lips) of her vagina, gently pulling it and letting it go in a rhythmic manner. Begin at the lower end and work your way up to the clitoris. When you've wibbled one outer lip, repeat the process on the other, and then move on to the inner lips.

CLITORAL MANOEUVRES
Using a well-lubricated finger, begin by circling the head of the clitoris at a steady pace, then change direction and circle in the opposite

FIRST MOVES
Before you begin the massage of your partner's genitals, lovingly stroke and pleasure the rest of her body.

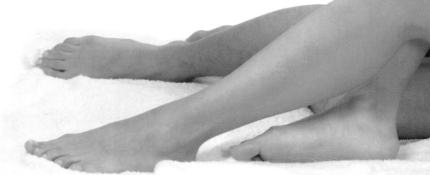

direction. Keep the pace even and regular. After 20 or so circles each way, rub the tip of your finger lightly up and down the side of the clitoris, 20 times on one side and then 20 times on the other. Now alter the stroke again and rub backward and forward immediately below the clitoris 20 times. Finally, still using that fingertip, rub from the clitoris down to the opening of the vagina and back 20 times.

There are many variations on all these strokes, and you might like to invent your own. But always ensure that your partner and your fingers are adequately oiled.

Wibbling
Start with one of the outer labia. Use both your hands at the same time, gently pull on it, then let go, just as you might do if this were one of the lips of your mouth.

Clitoral Manoeuvres
Extremely delicately, with an almost featherlight touch and using plenty of lubrication, run your finger first around the head and then up and down the shaft of her clitoris.

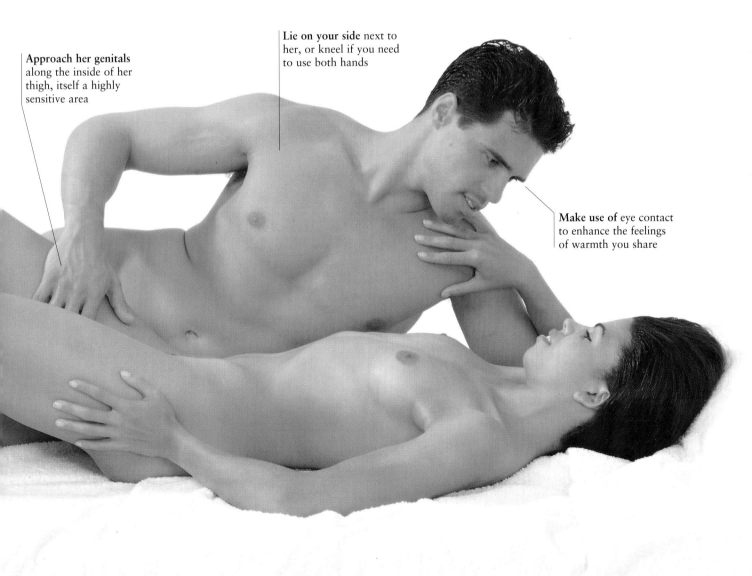

Approach her genitals along the inside of her thigh, itself a highly sensitive area

Lie on your side next to her, or kneel if you need to use both hands

Make use of eye contact to enhance the feelings of warmth you share

FOR HIS PLEASURE

When giving your man genital massage, remember that you are not aiming at bringing him to orgasm. If it happens, it's a bonus for him, but if not, it really doesn't matter, because you will still have given him wonderful sensations. These are the basic strokes I was originally taught, but there is nothing to prevent you from inventing a few of your own.

The Corkscrew
Put one hand on each side of the penis shaft. Slide them around in opposite directions at the same time – as if you were trying to twist the penis in half – and then slide them back again. Repeat ten times.

The Lemon Squeezer
Steady the penis by grasping it around the halfway mark with one hand. Then rub the cupped palm of your other hand over and around the head of the penis, as if you were juicing a lemon.

As with the massage for her pleasure *(see page 92)*, this ideally should not be used without massaging the rest of the body first. Without that whole-body build-up, it isn't anything like as effective. Begin by pouring a little warm oil into your hands and then liberally applying this to your partner's genitals, ensuring that his penis, testicles, and perineum are covered. Since this is a hairy area, use enough oil to allow your hands to slide around without catching.

THE COUNTDOWN
This consists of two strokes. For the first, grasp the top of his penis with your right hand and place your left hand underneath his testicles, with fingers positioned toward the anus. As you slide your right hand down the penile shaft, enclosing it as much as possible, bring your left hand up from his testicles. Aim to bring both hands slowly together at the base of the shaft.

For the second stroke, slide your right hand back up his penis from the base while simultaneously bringing your left hand back under his testicles again. As before, work slowly and steadily.

This is the basis of the count-down, with which you then go on to overwhelm your partner. The count goes as follows:
- ten times the first stroke, then ten times the second
- nine times the first stroke, then nine times the second
- eight times the first stroke then eight times the second, and so on until you reach one stroke.

THE CORKSCREW
This basically involves rubbing the shaft of his penis between the palms of your hands. It really goes without saying that you need to do this gently, but don't be afraid of maintaining quite firm pressure.

THE LEMON SQUEEZER
In this stroke, you rub the head of his penis with your cupped hand. It helps if you close your eyes and actually feel your hand brushing across the surface. Circle very gently, moving your hand

first ten times clockwise and then a further ten times anticlockwise. Use steady strokes, rather than slow ones, and as you become adept at making them, you will find that they take on a particular rhythm.

HAND OVER HAND

Like the simple children's game of "hand over hand", where you repeatedly bring your hand from underneath the pile of hands and place it on top, never breaking the rhythm, this has to be performed pretty quickly. The aim is to keep up a continuous hand-over-hand movement so that the head of his penis remains uncovered for as little time as possible.

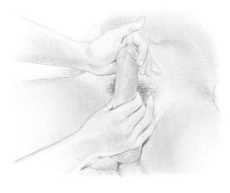

Hand over Hand
Slide your cupped hand over the head and down the shaft. Before it gets to the base, bring the other hand up to the head to repeat the stroke.

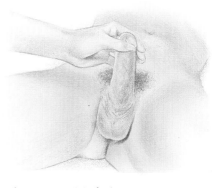

The Squeeze Technique
This is used to control ejaculation. If your partner tells you that he has the urge to ejaculate, grasp his penis and press your thumb against it just below the glans. Maintain firm pressure for ten seconds, or until his urge to ejaculate has subsided.

PERINEUM AND TESTICLES
Use your fingers and the palms of your hands to massage his perineum and, very gently, to fondle his testicles.

Be ready to use the squeeze technique to help your partner delay ejaculation

Let your partner know if you would like her touch to be lighter or firmer, faster or slower

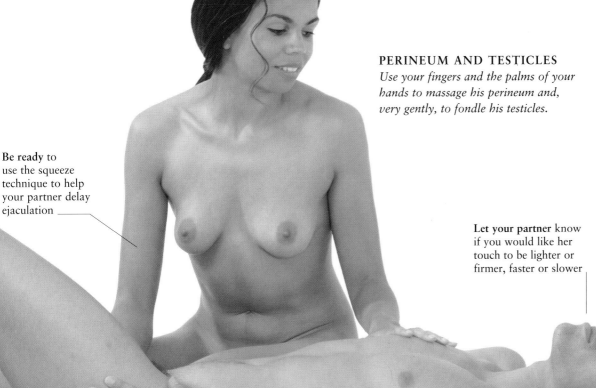

SELF-TOUCH TECHNIQUES

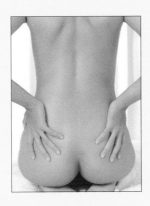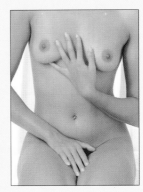

If you learn to love and understand your own
body, you are unlikely to develop inhibitions
about it that may make it difficult for you to
respond fully to sexual touch. By exploring
your body, you build up knowledge of its
responses, and of your own likes and dislikes,
that you can convey to your partner.

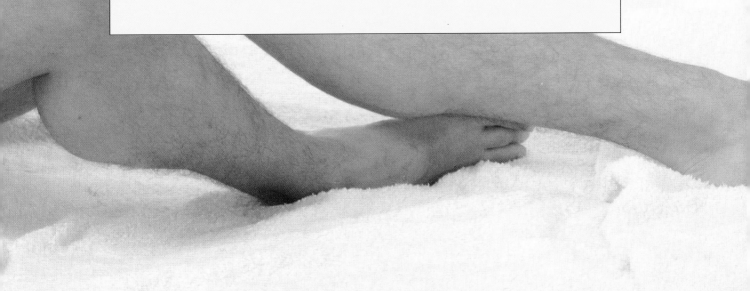

USING SELF-TOUCH

We can't all be fortunate enough to have a partner, and some of us prefer to live alone. This does not mean that we want to be starved of sensual touch, nor that we lose our sensuality or the desire to develop as sexual beings. In such circumstances, a sensual self-touch routine can help us maintain our sexuality, but such a routine can also be used to enhance a sexual relationship.

As we grow up, we consciously identify our sexual needs as well as unconsciously craving closeness, and we learn to look for specific sexual sensations – men more so than women. Because their genitals are so easy to find, and because they so naturally learn how to stimulate themselves, men usually develop their genital sensation as the main focus of their sensuality.

This means that when it comes to building a physical relationship with a woman, male genital sensation often comes into conflict with female all-over body sensation. It's important to say here that neither is "right": men and women have different spontaneous routes to sexual development.

One of the great benefits of this difference in sexual focus is that, as we become more educated about sex and more conscious of these differences, we can learn from each other. We can deliberately set out to gain new sexual perspectives from our partners that enrich our own sensual lives and almost certainly increase our mutual enjoyment of lovemaking.

But we can also enlarge our sexual horizons on our own. We can explore new aspects of sensuality for our own pleasure, and by developing sides to sexual selves that are more commonly ascribed to the opposite sex, we are likely to become better lovers.

SELF-TOUCH FOR WOMEN

In the sexuality workshops I used to hold for women, the ages of the participants ranged from 17 to 60. Most of them attended because they had never experienced orgasm, although one or two of them had managed it by accident or in their sleep. There were, in this diversity of the female sex, a number of common denominators. The first was ignorance of the body, the genitals, and sexual response. The second was a shared sense of isolation. The third was a

SELF-ESTEEM
One of the aims of self-loving is to boost your self-esteem by making you feel less solitary and more treasured – especially by yourself.

Lovingly fondle and squeeze your breasts and nipples

Explore the sensual potential of your pubic region and genitals

Run your fingers along your thighs and over your buttocks lack of confidence. By working even on only one of these issues, their lives improved immeasurably.

The methods I used in my group were based on a combination of group therapy styles originating in the USA under the separate auspices of Lonnie Barbach and Betty Dodson. Betty was my main influence, and the self-touch techniques for women that I describe are my own interpretation of Betty's inspired routines.

SELF-TOUCH FOR MEN

Men, in the Western world and Western tradition, are often starved of touch from an early age. There is the misbelief that this is part of a "toughening-up" process that boys must receive in order to prepare them for the rigours of the cruel outside world.

This may have been true back in an age when survival depended on being impervious to the elements and to the grind of backbreaking manual labour. Then again, it may not. In many Eastern cultures, men have traditionally been allowed far more sensuality as boys and young men than they have in the West. Yet they survived notwithstanding and were still masculine enough to beget children. Lack of touch is definitely not necessary to modern life. On the following pages, therefore, I propose a self-loving routine to help men use the whole body as an erogenous zone and thus further whole-body responses. This should extend your sensuality and enrich your life.

LEARNING ENJOYMENT
It is sadly easy to feel alone, even if you are committed to a partner. You can combat this lonely feeling by learning to enjoy self-touch.

Explore the ways your breasts and nipples react to touch

Experiment with different ways of stimulating your genitals

Locate the most sensitive areas of your upper thighs

CASE HISTORY
PHIL AND SELF-TOUCH

When Phil, aged 36, joined our women's group, she had never touched her genitals, nor had they ever been touched by the men who had been her lovers.

She concealed, beneath a sophisticated, well-groomed, woman-of-the-world style, a deep reticence and insecurity, but she flowered under our programme of self-touch. She began to look prettier, the result of relaxing about her sexuality, and became a truly sensual woman thanks to the power of her own fingertips.

SELF-TOUCH FOR MEN

For this routine, arrange to have at least an hour of uninterrupted privacy. Begin by giving yourself a warm bath or shower. A bath is preferable since it is a more relaxing experience and brings us closer to the days when we were floating in our mothers' wombs.

After your bath, move to a warm bedroom. Lock the door, and put up a do-not-disturb sign or let others in the house know that you are not to be interrupted. Place towels on your bed and lie down naked, with your back propped up by pillows, and begin the routine; the moves that are described below are illustrated on pages 102-103.

THE HANDS
Coat your hands with oil and rub them together. Note as you do the sensuality of palms slowly sliding around each other – close your eyes if it helps. Next, massage the back of each hand. What does the skin feel like? Is it soft, firm, gnarled? Next, go over the backs again with your fingertips. Note the difference in sensation as a result of the difference in touch. Now switch to the other hand and compare the sensations. Do both hands produce the same reactions? Is one more sensitive than the other?

THE ARMS
Now pour a little more oil into your palms and coat your forearms. Begin by rubbing the oil well in, using powerful whole-hand strokes, and then switch to something more loving. Think of your arm as if it were a lover's. Be gentle with it. Stroke it, caress it, brush your fingertips over the surface. Now repeat the exercise on the upper arm, and then on your other arm.

THE CHEST AND NIPPLES
Using the same technique of contrasting firm and gentle strokes, stroke the other parts of your body (don't forget that hairy areas need extra oiling to make them suitably slippery). Let your hands experience what it feels like to massage a male chest – this is what your lover feels when she massages you.

Coat your nipples with oil and stroke them gently to see what this feels like. Close your eyes again and imagine that it's a beautiful woman who's stimulating you. Perhaps you will feel sexually aroused by this mental picture, but don't give in to the temptation to move your hands down to your genitals. Be patient, and work on your abdomen instead.

THE ABDOMEN
This is an area where many people are ticklish, but even the most ticklish can be tamed with a firm touch. Once you've relaxed beneath your firm touch you may then surprise yourself by being able to enjoy a lighter one.

THIGHS, LOWER LEGS, AND FEET
When you massage your thighs and lower legs, note the level of touch that feels most arousing, and as you carry on touching, build on the erotic pricklings and see if you can enlarge these sensations without yet touching your genitals. Once again, you might like to imagine that a beautiful lover is caressing you.

The foot is one of the most fertile areas for self-massage. Pay special attention to those erogenous zones between the toes. Give them the most amazing and sensual treat of their hardworking lives.

THE BUTTOCKS
Lie on your side or your belly and stroke your buttocks with your fingertips, noting if there is more or less sensation near the anus and the perineum. If it were your lover caressing you, how would you like her to do it? Imagine you are her and direct your hands accordingly.

THE PENIS

Roll around again so that you are lying on your back once more, but propped against the pillows. As you stroke your penis, note how its surface feels to your touch. Return to the image of your sensual lover. What would she do to your penis?

Would she explore it by manipulating your foreskin? Would she rub her palm up and across your scrotum, before reaching your erection? Would she rub your penis harder than you do? What else might she do as she gives you a firmer grasp? Try speeding up your stroke without making it harder, then try slowing down but grasping more firmly still. As you end in orgasm, continue to visualize your woman's hands around you.

AFTERMATH

What feelings rose to the surface for you, during this exercise? Were you able to accept it unconditionally and forge ahead with enjoyment? Or did you feel uncomfortable, or devoid of any real sensation? Think about these latter if they apply to you. Where might the discomfort, or the

Harry's Experience

When I was a small boy, a teacher caught me masturbating and punished me severely. The humiliation was so extreme that I forced myself not to have sexual responses again. This, of course, made life very difficult when I got married. I could manage intercourse, but felt virtually

nothing. I eventually consulted a sex therapist, who encouraged me to reawaken my sexuality by means of self-pleasuring. It took determination, but things did change for me, and several weeks later I had a new pattern of sexual response – and a revitalized marriage.

lack of feeling, have come from in the first place? Why might you be blocking off pleasure? If you do have these uneasy feelings, try the exercise several more times in order to feel familiar with it and therefore more comfortable. And if it might help, talk this through later, with a friend.

You are attempting, by caressing your body, to bring to life nerve endings that have been hardly used. Just as you learned, all those years ago, that your penis possessed sensation, so too can you learn about other, more delicate feelings that are there to be developed and enjoyed.

PREPARATION

Ensure that you have absolute privacy, and begin by taking a warm bath to relax. This relaxation will help to clear your mind of outside troubles so that you can concentrate on, and enjoy, the self-touch routine that follows.

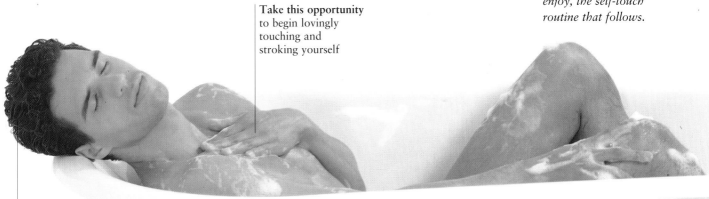

Take this opportunity to begin lovingly touching and stroking yourself

Lie back and relax in the enfolding warmth

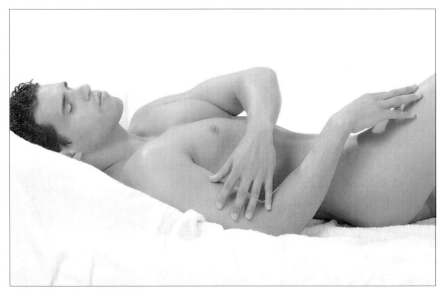

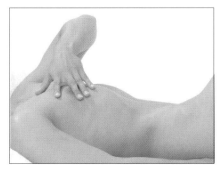

The Chest and Nipples

Apply the massage oil with both hands and move them in circles all over your chest except on the nipples, covering a small area at a time. Then apply a little fresh oil to each of your nipples, and gently stroke, squeeze, and fondle them to find out what it feels like.

The Hands and Arms

Begin by pouring a little warmed oil into your hands and massaging it from one hand to the other. Next, massage the back of each hand, noting the texture you are touching, then move on to your arms. Use powerful strokes up and down each arm, then squeeze the arm by the wrist and push your hand up to the elbow. Follow these firm strokes with more gentle touching.

The Abdomen

Oil your hands and move them firmly in circles over your abdomen, repeatedly working down from your waist to your groin and back up again. Then repeat, using a lighter action.

Cover your bed with towels to protect it from the massage oil

Make short, circular strokes with your fingertips and palms

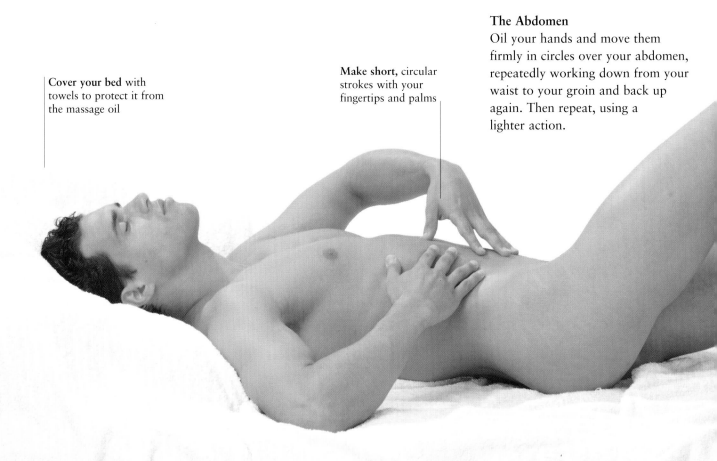

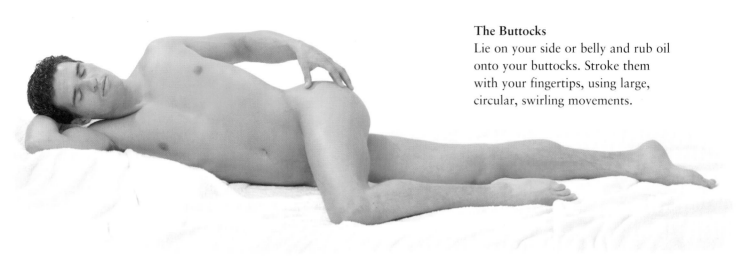

The Buttocks
Lie on your side or belly and rub oil onto your buttocks. Stroke them with your fingertips, using large, circular, swirling movements.

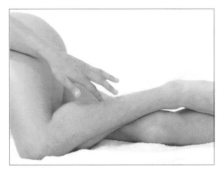

The Thighs
Stroke repeatedly from your knees up to your genitals, covering both the outsides and the insides.

The Lower Leg
Stroke each leg in turn, working repeatedly from the ankle up to the knee and back.

The Penis
Stroke your penis, but not as you would during masturbation. Note how your penis feels to your hand.

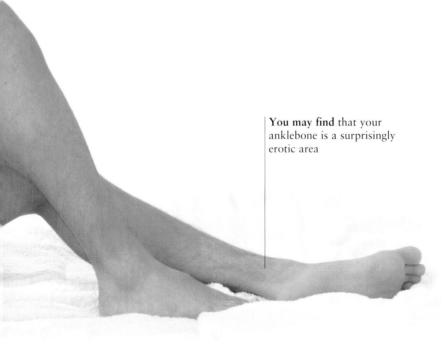

You may find that your anklebone is a surprisingly erotic area

THE FEET

Remember to include your feet in this self-touch routine. When you are working on them, you will find – if you are supple enough – that it is possible to use most of the basic foot-massage techniques that you would normally use on a partner *(see page 35)*.

SELF-TOUCH FOR WOMEN

This erotic self-touch routine is a highly pleasurable way of exploring your own body and getting to know and love it. By indulging yourself in such an intimate and sensuous fashion, you will be discovering your own likes and dislikes when it comes to sensual touch.

Begin by treasuring yourself. This sounds embarrassingly corny and therefore difficult to do, but it's worth trying. Look at yourself in a mirror and say, out loud, "I love you." Then embellish this: tell yourself, "You're terrific and I think you're wonderful." And look at yourself as if you love yourself, perhaps by smiling, or by looking seductive or passionate. And when, in future, you start being hard on yourself, stop for a minute, give yourself a hug, and say, "You're OK. I love you." Try to do this exercise two or three times a day for a month – you'll be pleasantly surprised at how much better you begin to feel.

A SENSUAL SHOWER

Give yourself a treat in the comforting warmth of a good shower *(see opposite)*. Lather yourself sensuously with your favourite shower gel and imagine it is your lover's hands that are doing the touching. He thinks your body is wonderful and his hands roam lovingly over your soapy crevices, caressing and teasing. Sometimes you wriggle away from his touch, but often his exploring hands hit the mark so well that you can hardly move while he takes advantage of your breathlessness.

Now that he has cornered you and is touching your genitals, lean on the shower wall and let yourself go with whatever moves your hands choose to make as they slide across your genitals, making them more and more slippery and sensitive. Sometimes they go slow and sometimes their movements get very fast indeed. Have fun being your own lover.

SELF-MASSAGE

Go in for this as if it were a massage with a partner. Prepare the room so that it provides you with a sensual background *(see page 64)*. If you can, position yourself in front of a mirror so that you see your oily hands lightly sliding across your body and exploring your own contours.

Be aware of areas of tense muscle and try to wriggle and relax them. Massage them firmly if it helps, letting your body yield to the pressure of your hands. If tension persists, try relieving it with the tense/relax method, which involves tensing your muscles hard for a count of five before letting go again. Relax the muscles in your face and mouth, and wriggle your neck, your arms, and your waist to make sure that all of these are loosened up.

Then begin your massage *(see page 106)*, starting at your head. Slowly rub, circle, and knead your way down to your chest and breasts, then work your way down your abdomen and pass on to your thighs, legs, and feet.

In your foot massage, use your thumbs and knuckles when you are working on the soles, and the tips of your thumbs when massaging between the tendons on the tops of the feet. Remember to include your toes in your foot massage.

CASE HISTORY

SUE AND SELF-PLEASURING

When Sue arrived at one of my workshops she was depressed and shy. Her last relationship had ended over two years before, and since then she had not been touched, affectionately or in any other way. During our group massage training she found pleasure for the first time in years. She felt that maybe she had some value as a human being after all and, from the self-pleasuring routine she carried out at home, she learned that she was orgasmic, and felt real hope for herself.

GENITAL PLEASURING

Move last to your genitals, massaging and caressing them in the same way that you did the rest of your body. Try looking at them in a mirror. Can you visualize them as a flower? Is it possible to arrange your labia into a flower shape? Seek the grace and beauty that exist within them.

Now spread your labia back so that you can see the interior clearly. Can you identify your clitoris and the hood around it, and below it the tiny urethra and the entrance to your vagina? Gently place your finger inside your vagina and note the texture of its interior. Can you reach to the far end where you can touch the tip of your cervix? Can you find the G-spot, which is thought to be located on the front wall of the vagina, some way toward the far end?

Try moving your finger around the inside of your vagina. What sensation does this give you? Note where there is more feeling and where there is less. Try putting your finger at the 12 o'clock position (the part of your vagina nearest the clitoris) and crooking it slightly. How does this feel? Try running your fingertip around the entrance to the vagina.

Now move your lubricated finger up to your clitoris and see if you prefer the finger circling on the clitoral head itself, or around it, or on either side. Or perhaps you like it on all these spots?

Continue with your genital exploration, building on the good sensations, giving yourself more of these, and letting yourself go to the rhythm of your fingers. Just pay attention to the range of feelings you are experiencing, however small. The aim is to build on these, and to make connections between your brain and your genitals that are strictly pleasurable.

At this stage you might like to enhance your genital stimulation by using a vibrator instead of your fingers. But if, with either fingers or vibrator, you feel yourself approaching climax, try to stave it off. Try to keep yourself on the brink of climax for about 15 to 30 minutes.

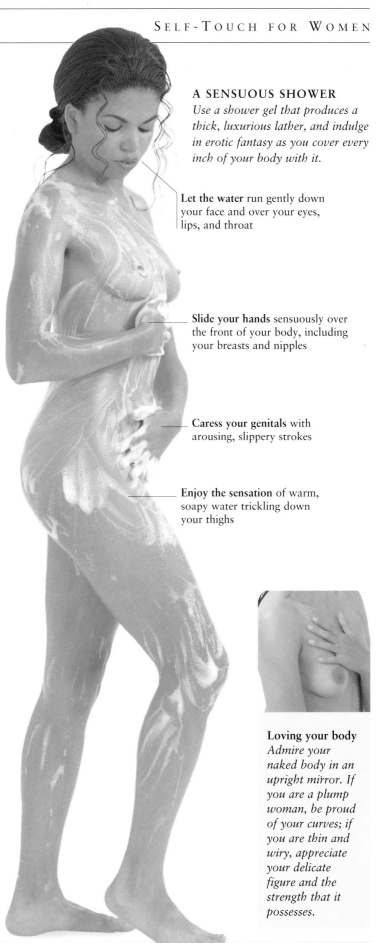

A SENSUOUS SHOWER

Use a shower gel that produces a thick, luxurious lather, and indulge in erotic fantasy as you cover every inch of your body with it.

Let the water run gently down your face and over your eyes, lips, and throat

Slide your hands sensuously over the front of your body, including your breasts and nipples

Caress your genitals with arousing, slippery strokes

Enjoy the sensation of warm, soapy water trickling down your thighs

Loving your body
Admire your naked body in an upright mirror. If you are a plump woman, be proud of your curves; if you are thin and wiry, appreciate your delicate figure and the strength that it possesses.

Arms
Pour a little oil into the palms of your hands and coat your forearms with it. Work it well into the skin, using powerful strokes, then stroke your forearms gently and lovingly with your fingers. Now repeat the exercise on your upper arms.

Experiment with different types of stroke to find out which are most pleasurable

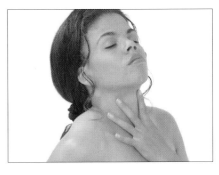

Neck and Throat
Give your hands a generous coating of oil, then gently stroke, fondle, and caress your neck and throat with your fingers and fingertips, and with the palms of your hands.

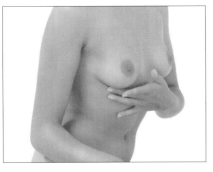

Gently tickle your nipples as they grow erect

Breasts
With warm, well-oiled hands, fondle and caress your breasts and move them in circles, paying attention to the bottoms and sides as well as to the tops and fronts. Then gently knead and squeeze them, first one at a time and then both together. Note which kind of touch feels best.

Nipples
Coat your nipples and areolae with massage oil and, using your fingertips, trace delicate circles on and around them.

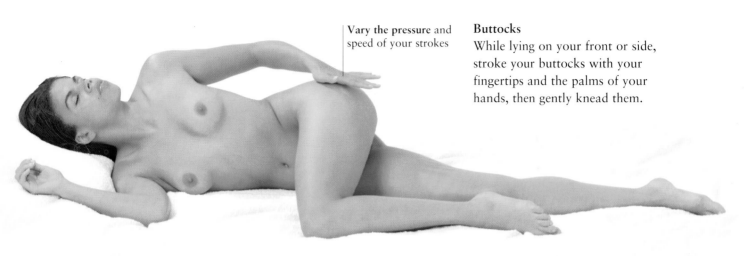

Vary the pressure and speed of your strokes

Buttocks
While lying on your front or side, stroke your buttocks with your fingertips and the palms of your hands, then gently knead them.

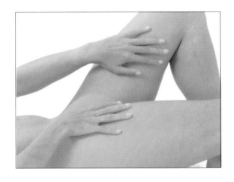

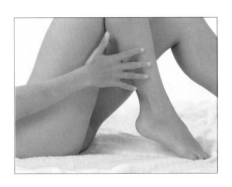

Insides of the Thighs
After massaging your buttocks, roll over onto your back and, without touching your genitals, stroke and fondle the insides of your thighs.

Outsides of the Thighs
Roll onto one side and massage the outside of your uppermost thigh. Then roll onto your other side and repeat on the other thigh.

Calves
Lie on your back and run your hands up the backs and sides of your calves, squeezing gently with your fingers and thumbs.

Genitals
Finally, lovingly caress and fondle your genitals. Explore them with your fingers, starting with the labia and vagina and then moving on to stimulate your clitoris.

Lie on your side or on your back

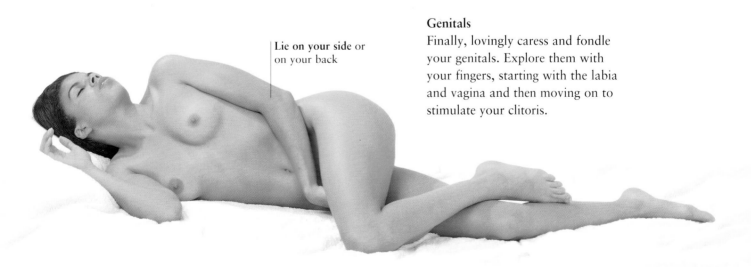

TOUCH *for* LIFE CHANGES

Important changes that occur in our lives and those of our partners, such as the birth of a child, the menopause, or male performance loss, can adversely affect our sensuality. Yet these effects can usually be mitigated by warmth, understanding, and, very often, by sensual touch and gentle, reassuring massage.

TOUCH FOR LIFE CHANGES

For many years, sex researchers have been trying to discover the exact nature of sexual desire, and to find out why, so often, it does not last. These questions have yet to be answered, but one thing we do know is that flagging interest in sex can often be overcome by employing the power of sensual touch.

The difficulty with living in a fast-moving, urbanized technological society is that we tend to lose touch with the natural rhythms of life. For example, we have developed efficient and reliable electric lighting, and so our activities no longer need be curtailed by the darkness of the night. Because we have central heating and air conditioning to keep us comfortable, and freezers in which to store our food all year round, we are much less affected by the changes of the seasons than our ancestors were. Unfortunately, being able to distance ourselves from the external rhythms of Nature has also led us to try ignoring our internal rhythms and patterns, particularly those that are related to growing older.

As little children, we are blessed with a store of apparently boundless energy. That energy takes on different but hectic patterns in adolescence, remains abundant in our twenties and starts to wind down slowly when we reach our late thirties. By the time we reach fifty, we may still feel young inside, but bits of our body just don't work in the ways they used to. And when we reach old age, unless we have – exceptionally – kept fit, we are most likely to be slow and stiff.

I'm stating the obvious here for one very good reason, and that is that no one ever expects the aging process to be reflected in his or her sex life (although many people think, erroneously, that sexual activity ceases in old age). Few people make allowances for the fact that ill-health and old age affect our sexual capabilities, as do (for women) pregnancy, nursing a baby, menstruation, and the menopause.

UNCERTAINTY
Major life changes can often create uncertainty, which in turn can lead to feelings of loneliness and isolation.

LACK OF DESIRE
One of the great mistakes of the so-called sexual revolution of the 1960s was that it taught us to treat our bodies like machines that never wear out. But our bodies react sensitively to the natural changes in our lives, and nowhere is this reflected more sharply than when we make love.

There are times in our lives when it is perfectly normal not to feel sexual desire, not to want to take part in the sex act, and not to need any sexual release. There is nothing wrong in feeling these things when there are good reasons to do so. They do not mean that we are lacking or wanting in any way, and it's a tragedy that we have somehow come to think we are.

SENSUAL RESPONSE

The response that doesn't change and remains steadfast throughout these sexual fluctuations is the sensual one. If you are someone who, on feeling the touch of a lover's hand, reacts with sensuality, you will probably continue to do so regardless of your age and the state of your health. Indeed, because touch is comforting as well as sensual, we probably need it far more than we need sex.

TOUCH PATTERNS

This section of the book concentrates therefore on special touch patterns and rites that help us through some of the more tricky stages of life. These will not, however, work effectively if they are used in isolation. If they are to be of any real value, you should combine them with the kind of basic, everyday loving touch that helps to keep any relationship on track.

In addition, if your partner is going through a major life change, he or she is liable to feelings of uncertainty and insecurity. You may need to show a great deal of sympathy, understanding, and reassurance, which you should always combine with good, old-fashioned, tender loving care.

ANDRE'S LACK OF INTEREST

Andre and his partner, Wendy, were in their late forties. Their sex life had ground to a halt, and I recommended that they try a programme of mutual touching and masturbation. It was remarkably successful – each of them was able to climax and they felt happy and closer together. The therapy never went any further than that. It did not need to: Andre simply didn't want intercourse, and the final counselling session ended with Wendy saying that she was so overjoyed by their renewed closeness that she did not need it either.

A STRONGER RELATIONSHIP
When you work together to overcome the difficulties created by life changes, you can strengthen the bonds of love that underpin your relationship.

Be open and honest with each other

Set aside time to spend in each other's arms

MENSTRUATION

Between the ages of about 13 and 50, women are subject to monthly menstrual cycles. Each month, they undergo the physical manifestations of ovulation and of shedding the lining of the uterus. These physical changes are accompanied by changes in various hormone levels, and since our moods are affected by our hormones, it means that we women tend to experience our emotions on a cyclical basis, too.

Headaches that occur during the menstrual cycle can be relieved by mild painkillers such as ibuprofen

The best way to discover just what your monthly emotional pattern consists of is to keep a menstruation diary. Over two or three months, chart not just your physical changes during menstruation but your emotional ones too, noting on which day in the cycle they occur. This information will show you clearly how your moods tend to

MENSTRUAL SYMPTOMS
Hormonal changes in the second half of the menstrual cycle can cause a number of adverse effects, such as headaches and tender breasts.

alter during your menstrual cycle, for instance whether you become ebullient or depressed, creative or negative. When you can predict how you will be feeling you can, if necessary, alter your behaviour to compensate for it.

MENSTRUATION AND TOUCH
The hormonal fluctuations of menstruation can affect how a woman experiences touch. Before I made the experiment of keeping a menstruation diary, I thought of myself as a sex queen, ever ready for sexual contact, but the information I gained from keeping the diary gave me a rude awakening.

My diary showed that on the day and the evening before my menses my skin felt marvellous. If you touched or stroked me on those occasions, every tiny, featherlight touch thrilled through me. My entire body could be set on fire with eroticism. In fact, this touch was better than the climax when it arrived. If I missed out on sexual touch on this magic day, I would have to wait another month before such wonders became available once more.

That didn't mean that I had no other erotic sensation. During the first ten or 12 days of each menstrual month, I was extremely receptive to touch. I was open,

❝ *Anne's Experience*

On one evening, a massage trainer decided my appalling premenstrual tension and early cramps could be wiped out by a good massage. Feeling almost twisted out of shape by tension, I demurred. I didn't want a massage – I knew I would be better off with a half-mile swim. But she insisted. Against my better judgement, I gave my body over to her. What followed was one of the most uncomfortable

experiences I've ever had. The massage hurt. The tension was not only not relieved, it was greatly exacerbated. It was the perfect example of how not to tune in to your subject. As a direct result of this experience, I worked out a much more useful way of alleviating pre-menstrual tension and of building on what sensuality your swollen tissues and cramped muscles will allow through. ❞

BUILDING ON SENSITIVITY

Relaxation

Paradoxically, by increasing tension you can eventually relax. A long swim or a jog that uses up all your spare energy will help. If you don't enjoy physical exercise, a good alternative is to put yourself through the tense/relax exercise *(see page 29)*.

Physical warmth

Many women (but not all) find that physical warmth helps them to relax. If you have a loving partner, ask him to cuddle you. If you don't have a partner, you might find that a hot-water bottle is an acceptable substitute.

Back massage

A back rub, in which he squeezes the pressure away from the base of your spine *(see page 68)* may be invaluable. But the golden rule is to give your partner feedback, telling him what feels good and what does not.

Light touch

When a firm touch feels uncomfortable, ask your partner to try a light, fingertip touch, which might float over your skin and transform the tension into eroticism. If your discomfort is metamorphosed in this way, lovemaking and orgasm may be therapeutic. But be aware that sometimes even a light touch can be irritating.

relaxed, full of energy, and highly sexual. Then, for 48 hours, my body would feel as if it had been hit by a truck. I would be too tired to cook supper, let alone overwhelm my lover by taking the sexual initiative. My body was probably ovulating at this time.

Afterwards, although I was capable of being sexual and having orgasms, I got tetchier and more irritable as the end of the menstrual month approached, and given a choice, wouldn't initiate sex. Yet when I was at my tetchiest, around Day 26, I would revert to being highly sexual. The tension generated could be translated into

energy, both creative and sexual. I thus discovered that for almost the full second half of my menstrual month I would not have minded in the least if I did not have sex. It was a shock.

But knowing about this pattern enabled me to improve my sex life. The first half of the month didn't need much alteration. During the exhausting days of ovulation, I left sex well alone, but during the second half of the month, I knew that to be truly aroused I needed strong stimulation and my man needed to take the initiative. I ended up calmer and more sure of myself.

WARM CUDDLES
For relaxing warmth, ask your partner to cuddle you in a "spoons" position. This is one in which you lie on one side and he lies behind you, snuggled up against your back.

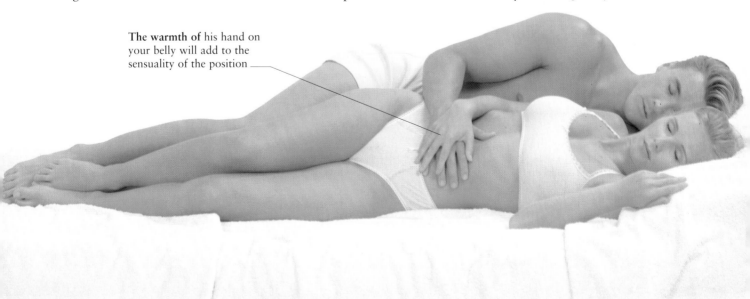

The warmth of his hand on your belly will add to the sensuality of the position

PREGNANCY

Pregnancy, especially first pregnancy, is a time in life when everything changes for the expectant couple, above all their relationship. As the woman grows larger, her partner sees her as a mother. The shift from lover to mother and back again can be disconcerting and difficult to deal with. While it's not difficult to feel sexual toward a lover, it can be hard if you suddenly start viewing her as a parent.

A woman's view of her partner may also change. In most families, the man's financial role assumes greater importance – at least for a while. For perhaps the first time in the relationship, the woman becomes financially dependent on her partner. This may, in her eyes, give him an uneasy power over her, but he might feel the increased responsibility as a heavy burden.

These shifting pressures interrupt the process of relating and loving, and this is commonly the time when husbands seek love and affection elsewhere; it's not unknown for pregnant women to do the same. Pregnancy is a time of emotional fluctuation for most women, because their hormones, and therefore their moods, are not at their normal levels.

After the birth, a woman's breastfeeding – or lack of it – will influence her sex drive (see page 116). The extreme emotions that childbirth brings forth may mean poignant passion between husband and wife that nevertheless, for physical reasons, is not expressed sexually.

LOVING TOUCH

One of the most important practical moves that a man and his partner can make at this time is literally to stay in touch. Loving touch reinforces the bonds between the partners, to their mutual benefit, but it is doubly important to the pregnant woman. Clinical observation has shown that a woman who is lovingly touched before her baby is born, and during childbirth, is more likely to be physically demonstrative toward her baby than is a woman who has not received such touch.

Massage during pregnancy is an excellent addition to every-day touching, cuddling, and kissing as a means of maintaining the loving bonds between a couple. Most of the strokes used in

FINGERTIP MASSAGE
One of the most useful massage techniques to use on your pregnant partner is making light, circling strokes with your fingertips.

Use one hand to steady your partner, the other one to massage her

Massage her arms, back, and belly

ordinary massage will also work well for pregnant women, but some of them are especially pleasing.

MASSAGE STROKES

The base of the spine bears a lot of weight at the best of times, and when it's carrying an extra load – as it does in the last months of pregnancy – it becomes desperate for relief. Ordinary back massage strokes cannot, however, be used to relieve the tension, for fear of crushing the baby.

The next best alternative is for the woman to sit or kneel while her partner rubs her lower back gently but firmly with the palm of his hand. Using the thumbs for back massage also gets rid of extreme knots of tension. Some women find this back-pain relief wonderfully effective during labour, particularly when the contractions are experienced as backache.

A woman's legs also take the extra weight of the baby and if, by the end of the pregnancy, they are supporting an extra 13 kilos (28 pounds) or more, they can become full of fluid. Cramp in the legs is also common because the circulation of the blood is not as straightforward as it would be normally. The classic draining strokes for the legs *(see pages 84-87)* are ideal for this condition. Practise first on the lower leg and then on the thighs.

The classic circling stroke, such as that shown on page 66, can be used on all areas of the body, and fingertip strokes that brush the pregnant abdomen will stimulate the nerves on the surface of the skin and alleviate strain. When used during labour, stroking the abdomen can reduce the sensation of the contractions for some women, although I confess to finding it just maddening when it was done to me.

Another useful stroke is to rub warm massage oil gently into the perineum (the skin between the vagina and anus). This helps to make it supple, which will reduce the risk of it tearing during the delivery.

MASSAGE IN PREGNANCY

- When massaging a pregnant woman, ask for feedback to find out which spots to focus on and which to avoid
- Avoid putting any weight on or around the "bump"
- The mother-to-be needs to lie down in such a way that the "bump" feels comfortable and supported

BACK MASSAGE
By massaging her lower back, you can help to relieve the strain caused by the extra load she is carrying.

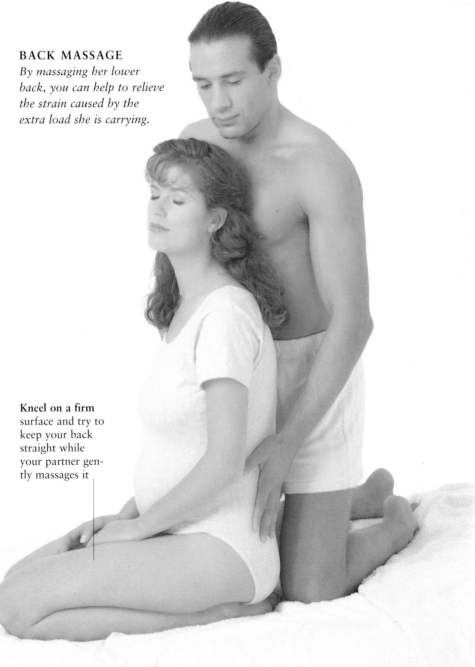

Kneel on a firm surface and try to keep your back straight while your partner gently massages it

AFTER THE BIRTH

What prospective parents are never told is that after the birth, the mother often feels as if she's been hit by a tornado. She may be able to totter about the house caring for the baby, but she won't be much good for anything else. Her partner, on the other hand, expects everything to get back to normal quickly and doesn't understand why life remains upside-down.

To begin with, if you get very little sleep, and the little you get is continually interrupted, you slow down, become forgetful, and feel like a robot. This does not make you the greatest of lovers, which is unfortunate because these early months are an emotive time. It's the first time in the relationship when the woman's attention isn't focused on the man. He feels the difference, and usually acts up.

Fingertip kneading is very effective in the neck and shoulder area

In addition, all that mothering makes a woman feel urgently in need of some mothering herself. In extended families living together or in the same neighbourhood, this mothering can be provided by the woman's mother or mother-in-law, but this arrangement is much less common than it once was. Most women have to cope without any extra help, so the weeks and months after the birth are a time of exhaustion at a stage when their emotions are always on edge. But some of these tired passions may lead to poignant lovemaking. What women lose in ease of sexual arousal (thanks to the very low levels of oestrogen in their bodies at this time), they gain in terms of emotions.

That low in oestrogen levels, with its concomitant lower energy levels, lasts for a long time. In addition, if a woman is breastfeeding she will also be producing the hormone prolactin, and one of its side-effects is to reduce sexual desire. When weaning begins and breastfeeding declines, the prolactin levels fall and sexual desire comes back. But I don't believe women regain their full energy again for at least a year after a birth.

Another problem that may arise is pain during intercourse, caused by a poor episiotomy (the surgical cutting of the vulva to facilitate the birth). If the woman has been sutured poorly after the birth, the scar can be very sensitive and this makes intercourse painful. (This discomfort fades with time, but some episiotomies are so poorly done that a new operation is needed to cut out the scar tissue and give the area a chance to heal normally.)

NECK STROKES
Using kneading strokes plus fingertip kneading, work across the shoulders from the sides and up the neck into the hairline, then work down the neck and across to the sides again. Repeat as often as your partner wishes.

OVERCOMING ALIENATION

Such physical and emotional problems make this a time when it is easy for the couple to feel alienated from each other. Anything that can build a bridge between them is therefore of great value. Touch can be such a bridge and massage a large part of the supporting structure. The touch needs to be one-way during this time – in her direction. But she can repay him later with some very special sexual treats when her desire and energy have returned.

SOOTHING MASSAGE

To ease your partner's tired muscles and help her to relax, give her a soothing back massage and finish off with neck strokes, forehead circling, and a temple press *(see opposite and below)*.

Start off with a back rub. With your partner lying face-down, hold the side of her body with one hand. With your other hand, rub in circles around the base of her spine with a deep, firm pressure. Change hands and repeat the move, then circle with both hands together. Follow this with thumb pressure. Using the pads of both thumbs, circle deeply and firmly on either side of her spine, between her waist and the base of her spine.

MASSAGE FOR FATHERS

Reward your partner's loving attention by giving him a sensual treat once you have got your strength back – make a special occasion out of giving him a whole body massage that culminates in a genital massage. You might like to begin by bathing him as if he were a baby, drying him in hot fluffy towels, feeding him delicious fruits and wine, and generally making a fuss of him. Don't expect to have the energy to do this until at least three months after the birth.

Complete the back massage with heavier strokes. Place both hands on either side of your partner's spine, just below the waist, with your fingers pointing sideways and down toward her hips. Lean heavily on your hands, applying the pressure evenly and allowing the weight of your body alone to move your hands apart and down, as slowly as possible. They will slide apart, and when the stroke has ended, move them down the back slightly and repeat it until you have covered the area from the waist down to just above the tail of the spine.

Forehead Circling

Using the pads of your forefingers, make very tiny, gentle, circular strokes all over her forehead. Work from one side to the other and back again, varying the pressure and speed of the strokes as you go.

Temple Press

Place your palms on each side of your partner's forehead so that your fingertips just meet in the centre. Hold your hands lightly in place, press gently for a few seconds, then hold lightly again before lifting off.

Male Performance Loss

The decline in a man's sexual powers as he grows older is a rather different life change to the others in this chapter, such as the menopause *(see page 120)*, because it is a gradual process rather than a single, identifiable event. Every man experiences it differently, but there do seem to be common denominators, both emotional and physical, that many men share.

On the emotional side, there is the sense that time is passing, and that death is getting nearer (this may be accentuated by the death of a parent). A man may also feel that there may not be many years of optimum health left; that the pattern of life and his present love relationship are pleasantly but boringly familiar. On the physical side, there may be fears that potency is waning.

A man of 50 will probably need twice the penile touching and rubbing to stay erect and achieve an orgasm than a man of 30. He may find loss of hardness is a problem, as is loss of ejaculatory power and sensation. Whereas a boy of 17 will probably suffer from unwanted erections, the older man may need a lot of attention from a loving and skilful partner before he can get an

erection. He may also find one orgasm a day is his limit, possibly considerably less. Sex is like riding a bicycle: in good health, you can do it at any age, but you may take longer to arrive and have to pedal harder when you are older. But the journey is perhaps more pleasant if you don't rush, and the older lover can be the most satisfying.

It's important to stress that a "poor" relationship may be enough to prevent a man from getting an erection. However, the reverse is not necessarily true. If he fails to get an erection, that doesn't mean he's bored with his partner or wants to end the relationship – there may be a physical cause. We now know that perhaps 60 to 70 per cent of impotence cases have physical causes. The majority of these are curable, so a man who becomes impotent should always seek medical advice.

Hormonal changes

Although there is no hormonal menopause for men as there is for women, there is usually a gradual decline in the levels of the male sex hormone testosterone circulating in the bloodstream. Men reach their sexual peak at about the age of 18: their ability to be sexual, to feel desire, and to experience

Increasing His Response

- Oral sex, genital massage, and a great deal of masturbation with a firm hand are good starting points. Ask him for feedback. How might you increase the feeling? Could your strokes be rougher and harder?
- What about other aspects of increasing his arousal? Would using fantasy be helpful *(see page 126)*?
- Anal rimming, where you run your fingertip around just inside the rim of his anus, can be extremely arousing.

Discussing the Problem
Men are often reluctant to discuss their declining sexuality, because they mistakenly equate performance with masculinity.

satisfactory erection and orgasm are on the decline ever after. This isn't as tough as it sounds, though, because the decline is very gradual, and most middle-aged men are capable of powerful sensuality and wonderful orgasms – in the right circumstances. But most middle-aged men would agree that it takes longer to reach orgasm and that they need firmer direct stimulation.

Apart from declining testosterone levels, there are other aspects of aging that can affect sexual performance. Failure to achieve or maintain an erection, late-onset non-insulin-dependent diabetes, and the after-effects of prostate surgery are all instances of physical conditions that can impede the ability to have intercourse. Most men see their sexuality as an integral part of their personalities, and so they worry about such symptoms of aging.

An aging man's long-term partner may, of course, recognize that lovemaking isn't what it used to be and may encourage him to seek specialist advice. But very often, the pattern of a declining love life seems written in stone, and it takes a shift in mind-set to realize that sexual patterns can and should be altered. Be aware that you may still be capable of learning and adopting new lovemaking techniques, even after 25 years of the same routine.

With a new partner, the anxious male may feel it a burden to explain that he can't be as spontaneous as a young man. Most women, however, are highly tolerant of such differences and see new sexual needs as a challenge. If a man makes lyrical love to his partner with his

hands and tongue, bringing her up to and through a series of climaxes, she isn't going to mind too much about any sex aids or special attention he subsequently needs.

SPECIAL DESIRES
Ask your partner if he has any secret sexual needs or desires that you could share with him.

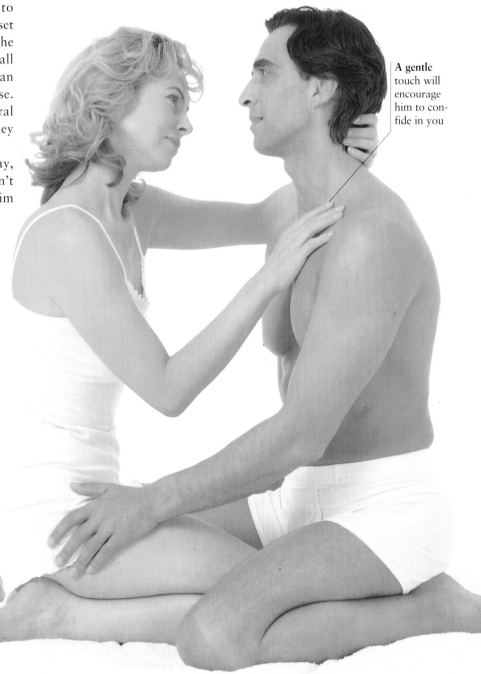

A gentle touch will encourage him to confide in you

THE MENOPAUSE

All women go through the menopause, but although not all of them experience a mid-life crisis, this can be a difficult stage in a woman's life. Just when physical changes in the body are making a woman feel older, more tired, and less attractive, not to mention anxious or depressed, children leave home and so, sometimes, do husbands.

On the debit side, many women feel totally unwanted as a result of all this. But on the credit side, some women feel healthier and more balanced emotionally than they have in years, and go on to tackle careers or courses of study with renewed vigour. Many couples greatly enjoy life together without the constant demands of a family, and rediscover each other as a result.

Complications can arise, however, if she meets with career success, possibly for the first time, while his career starts to wane or he has to take early retirement. Since his reaction may be to feel belittled, he may adopt aggression as a form of defence. His aggression may in turn upset how they relate to each other in bed, because neither may feel like encouraging the other and so their sex life deteriorates.

Physical changes may also make sex less satisfactory. For example, lower levels of the hormone oestrogen in the menopausal woman can lead to a lessening of vaginal

GIVING REASSURANCE
A sense of warmth and closeness is an invaluable gift to give to a menopausal partner, and will calm and reassure her.

Stroking and touching her will let her know that she is still valued and desired

lubrication. She may then find intercourse uncomfortable, and also that stimulation of her genitals doesn't work as effectively as before: post-menopausal women often need longer and more careful stimulation before they can climax. Hormone replacement therapy (HRT) and vaginal lubricants and pessaries can be very effective in overcoming this.

LIBIDO AND DEPRESSION

Lack of sexual desire is something else that becomes apparent after the menopause. Research shows that lovemaking often halts at around or after this time, at the instigation of the woman. One theory has it that as oestrogen levels wane in the menopausal woman so, too, do levels of testosterone, the hormone that many believe is responsible for libido. (Her partner might also be affected by reduced levels of testosterone *(see page 118)* and other aspects of aging.) Some menopausal women treated with extra testosterone report increased sexual drive, but this is sometimes accompanied by aggressive feelings that can prove destructive.

During this major life change, women need their partners to be especially understanding and sensitive. A useful rule that every man should remember is this: at any

" *Maureen's Experience*

When I started hormone replacement therapy, it didn't have an immediate result, but I did feel greatly improved after the second month. I spruced up my appearance and invested in two glorious massages. I paid attention to what was being done to me, then I made a date with my husband – in the bedroom. He was pretty intrigued, and he liked it even better when I undressed him, lovingly soaped him in a warm bath, then gave him a gorgeous massage. He actually volunteered to do the same for me after I'd finished with him and we ended by making love. I think we feel better about each other than we have for years. "

time when your partner seems abnormally volatile, ask yourself what may be going on inside her, and what may be the cause of it. Because the volatility can easily be directed toward you, it can be hard not to take her behaviour personally, but looking for other motives is always sensible.

One of the underlying characteristics of the menopause can be mild depression, so mild that many women who have it are unaware of it. But emotions are accentuated because of this depression, and acts of kindness will assume greater meaning. Giving a partner the treat of a massage when she hasn't expected it, or simply arranging to do something that is for her pleasure alone, becomes a loving act of great significance in these circumstances.

FOR HER PLEASURE

Give her an all-over body massage, carried out simply but sensitively. Ask if there are any particular spots of tension or pain, and do your best to stroke the tensions away. Then extend the massage to her genitals, but use a vaginal lubricant instead of massage oil when you start on them. Using some of the genital massage strokes *(see pages 92-3)*, begin to build up her sexual response.

Reapply the lubricant regularly. Let her feel bathed in it as your fingers explore first her labia and then her

clitoris. Establish a deliberate rhythm, brushing up against first one side of the clitoris and then the other. Make it clear that you have every intention of keeping this up for a long time.

Although it may take a menopausal woman longer to climax, when she does so, the climax is likely to be powerful because of the extended build-up. You can make this build-up even more intense by using a vibrator, but ensure that your lover's genitals and the end of the vibrator are both liberally coated in lubricant.

IMPROVING *the* EXPERIENCE

An easy way to improve the quality of a
sexual experience is by using fantasy. In your
imagination, you can be transported into any
erotic scenario that you, or your partner, can
devise. Another way is to counteract any
sensation blockers that are preventing you
from enjoying it to the full.

SEX IN THE BRAIN

The brain is perhaps the most powerful sex organ of all, because sexual thoughts have the power to create physical sensations within our bodies. For example, some men can rapidly achieve an erection simply by thinking intensely about an attractive woman, and some women fantasize so effectively that they can climax without a finger being laid upon their bodies.

Men and women whose sexual feelings have been dormant for years may find that their sexual responses suddenly blossom as the result of a chance encounter with someone whose imagination triggers theirs. Suddenly they're feeling like teenagers again because, for the first time in years, someone matches, indeed challenges, the far shores of their own fantasy worlds.

There are people who can chart a kind of personal sexual progress through what happens in their fantasy lives. Our fantasy lives often begin with dreams, frequently the first occasions on which boys and some

girls reach climax. Afterwards, we may remember the dream and unconsciously recreate the sexual scene within it. It is our first experience of fantasizing. As our sexual sophistication increases, so too does the content of our dreams and fantasies.

If we're lucky, we may find ourselves able to recount these fantasies to our lovers. Perhaps they, too, may be turned on by them, and help embellish the ideas so that we end up creating sexual stories jointly with our lovers. But when developing a relationship with a new lover, it can be disappointing to discover that his or her pattern of fantasizing is different. It feels as if a dimension is missing. Such differences are almost inevitable, however, but that missing dimension of shared fantasy can often be newly created.

FANTASY AND SURVIVAL

It's interesting to consider whether the ability to fantasize sexually has any human survival value. Humans have achieved as much as they have because they possess more curiosity and more imagination than any other of the great apes. We've conquered Everest, gone to the Moon, created life in test tubes, and learned to communicate from one side of the world to the other. All these achievements have been triggered by curiosity and imagination.

So where has sexual imagination taken us so far? And where are we going with it now? One theory is that we were designed

FANTASY AS COMPENSATION

Fantasy may be used unconsciously to compensate for imbalance in our daily lives. For instance, a judge may need the occasional break from his power and responsibility by being treated like a slave or an infant. His sexual fantasies may provide such an escape. A woman who has had powerful restrictions placed upon her expression of her sexuality may need to imagine being overpowered before she can respond fully to arousal. There is also an opposite case, where a woman who is powerful at work needs her partner to expose her inner frailties. But if he is unable to, she might then take refuge in dreams of seduction.

to have multiple sexual relationships within our original tribal groups, but that as the tribes became less communal and more diverse, we had to become monogamous in order to ensure the creation of succeeding generations. Because we were originally meant to be polygamous, all that sexual curiosity still had to go somewhere, and so the safeguard of polygamous sex in our imaginations appeared.

There's also my theory of boredom. Boredom seems to me to be a major threat to the kind of creative life we need if we are to develop as a species. If, through familiarity, we grow bored with our partners, we may no longer continue having sex and our relationships might disintegrate. Should we have no children, the line ends. If we do have children, the stable family unit needed for rearing them splits up. But when we are able to bring fantasy into our love lives, we continue in a relationship happily for years and our descendants are born, grow up, and eventually succeed us.

Sexual fantasies can be very beneficial to both men and women, whether they are used as a prelude to lovemaking, during intercourse, or during mutual or solo masturbation. They can, for instance, be used

to revitalize a sexual relationship that has grown stale and boring. They can also sometimes be of help to men with erectile problems, and to women who have difficulty becoming fully aroused.

INFINITE CHOICE
In a fantasy, either or both of you can pretend to be anyone you choose and do anything you want.

Use your hands to suggest restraint or domination

Combine your fantasies with sensuous touch, for instance stroking with a feather, to increase your partner's arousal

THE USE OF FANTASY

When I worked for *Penthouse Forum*, many of the lurid sexual exploits recounted in readers' letters were obviously and grossly fake, but some of them were borderline. They could have been real, or they could have been invented. We would invariably give the letter writers the benefit of the doubt because, even if the experiences described were fantasies, such fantasies were, we reckoned, legitimate aspects of sexuality.

But what about people who don't have sexual fantasies? I meet some of them in my women's sexuality workshops. These workshops are for women who so far are unable to experience orgasm. Many are helped by learning to fantasize, which they do by reading sexy literature and then, next time they are making love, visualizing the stories that aroused them. Other women in the same groups need only to be "given permission" to fantasize, and turn out to be able to do so without the help of books.

USING FANTASIES

Many people prefer to keep their fantasies for their own private use, because then they remain entirely personal. In addition, some people are very ashamed of their fantasies, while others fear that a fantasy will lose its eroticism if aired in public. A lot of people, however, like to talk their fantasies

through with a partner. Doing this can be such an act of trust that the relationship deepens. Another advantage shows up when you discover that your partner has corresponding or complementary fantasies. In these circumstances, your fantasies may be enriched and grow in eroticism, and can be used to develop sensational sex and remarkable love.

Going even further and acting out a fantasy can be a powerfully exciting adjunct to your sex life. There are many men and women who have played out fantasies such as picking each other up in bars, visiting hotel rooms wearing only fur coats *(see page 151)*, and making love outdoors *(see page 136)*. As long as these activities don't infringe on anyone else's privacy, don't harm anyone, and don't break any laws, they can be amazingly stimulating.

It is, of course, important to remember that if you feel you are being asked to do something that feels wrong, you should not hesitate to refuse. Also, it is a reasonable general rule that if your fantasy, or your partner's fantasy, involves any kind of violence, leave it well alone.

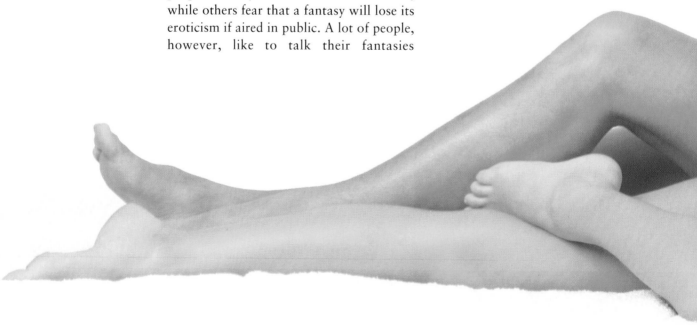

FANTASY SUGGESTIONS

Here are some ideas that show how you can create and develop simple sensual fantasies with your partner.

The circus
Take your listener among the artistes and the animals. What might be seen there? Try to keep the ideas sensual. For example, ask your partner to think about the costumes or the smell of the sawdust.

The sea
Describe a glimmering summer sea, the sight of it, the smell, the sensation of swimming in it. Visualize the pounding of the surf and water crashing onto rocks.

The magician's palace
Ask your partner to visualize being held prisoner in an ancient palace, stripped naked, and tied up in the dungeon.

RESTRAINT FANTASIES
A common theme in sexual fantasies is that of being physically restrained in some way. You can suggest the restraint of such a fantasy by loosely binding the wrists.

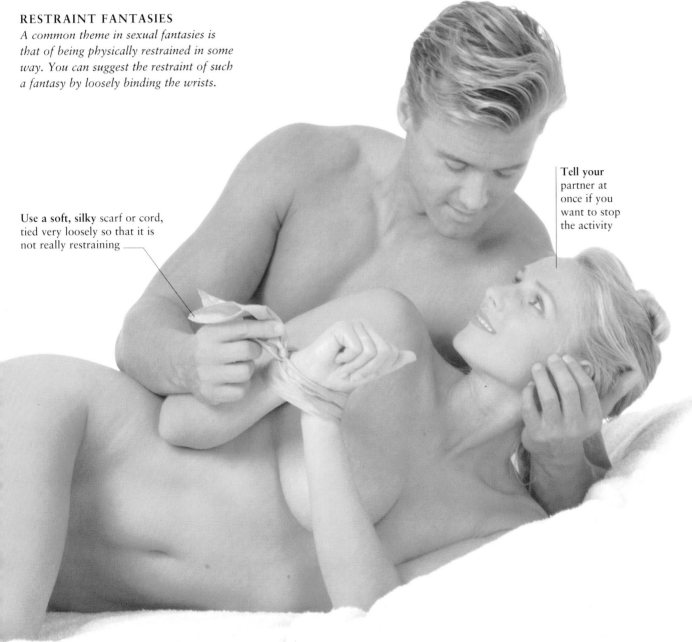

Use a soft, silky scarf or cord, tied very loosely so that it is not really restraining

Tell your partner at once if you want to stop the activity

MALE SENSATION BLOCKERS

I remember feeling puzzled, early in my massage studies, by occasionally coming across men who seemed to get little real enjoyment out of my tactile attentions. Yes, the sensation was pleasant, they'd concede, but it wasn't anything particularly special.

The men who said this were invariably the possessors of what felt like very solid flesh. Whenever I gave such a man a massage, I couldn't move his skin in ripples because it seemed to be fastened to one place. It felt to me as though powerful muscles beneath his skin were quite literally blocking the action of my hands, and also blocking any sensation for him.

It wasn't until I read about Wilhelm Reich's concept of "body armour" that I gained some insight into this problem. Reich's theory is that some people are permanently tense, and that this tension is expressed by unconsciously holding the muscles taut. The overall effect is that the tense person is wearing a layer of muscular armour to protect himself from the intrusions of the outside world.

What were the repercussions of this for making love, I wondered? Common sense told me that such a man would probably get little out of overall body contact and would instead be likely to focus all his sensuality on his penis, the one organ allowed to be "vulnerable". I checked this out by asking these men, and they agreed.

The answer offered by many professional masseurs is "rolfing". This is a form of very deep massage, invented by Dr Ida Rolf of Colorado. It is painful to receive, and when offered is usually combined with talking therapy: as the tension decreases, the person being massaged talks about what may have contributed to building up such barriers. Rolfing isn't something that can be done by amateur masseurs and it is best left to the professionals.

DRUGS

Other causes of male sensation blockers might be adverse reactions to certain drugs. Many of the drugs commonly used in the prevention and cure of illness can impair sexual performance, as can alcohol and illicit "recreational" drugs such as cocaine

PHYSICAL CAUSES OF SENSATION BLOCKERS

Sometimes, diseases or abnormal physical conditions of the body can reduce or destroy tactile sensation. Multiple sclerosis and other illnesses that affect the nerves are obvious culprits. Some localized conditions also affect sexual response. For example, nerve damage as the result of prostate operations may cause inability to achieve erections. Other possible causes of sexual dysfunction are pain caused by arthritis and anxiety as a result of asthma, which can result in the unconscious blocking of sexual signals from the brain to the genitals, and therefore of physical arousal.

General anaesthesia and surgery can be responsible for creating mild depression, which may in turn result in greatly lessened sexual desire. This situation usually improves in the months following surgery, but for some men even the suggestion that illness or surgery can impair their sexual feeling may actually be the cause of that loss of feeling. Many men with a more positive attitude do not suffer the same loss. Finally, diabetes affects erection but not desire, and sufferers can achieve great success with injection therapy that provides artificial erections.

(see pages 132-3). Alcohol is a brain depressant. In small amounts, it reduces anxiety and inhibition, and this may allow sexy feelings to emerge that otherwise would not be given the chance. In larger doses, however, alcohol rapidly impairs physical and mental functions, including sexual response, in both men and women. It reduces testosterone levels, and many men find it difficult to get an erection when they are drunk. Barbiturates and other hypnotic drugs have a similar action.

Antidepressant drugs have mixed effects on sensuality. They may bring back desire and sensual sensation after these have been dampened down by depression, but they also tend to impair the mechanics of orgasm. It is usually only by coming off antidepressants that a person can get his or her sexual desire, arousal, and performance fully back to normal again.

DISCUSSING IT

If a man is suffering from some sort of sensation block, he should discuss it frankly with his partner. Often, just talking about the problem will help to alleviate it.

CASE HISTORY
STEVE AND LOSS OF DESIRE

Steve's interest in sex with his partner, Naomi, was on the wane, and sometimes he could not even get an erection. When I asked him about his general health, he said that he had been taking an ulcer-healing preparation. I was able to reassure him that impaired sexual function was a common effect of the drug, and that when he had completed the course of treatment, his libido and potency would soon return.

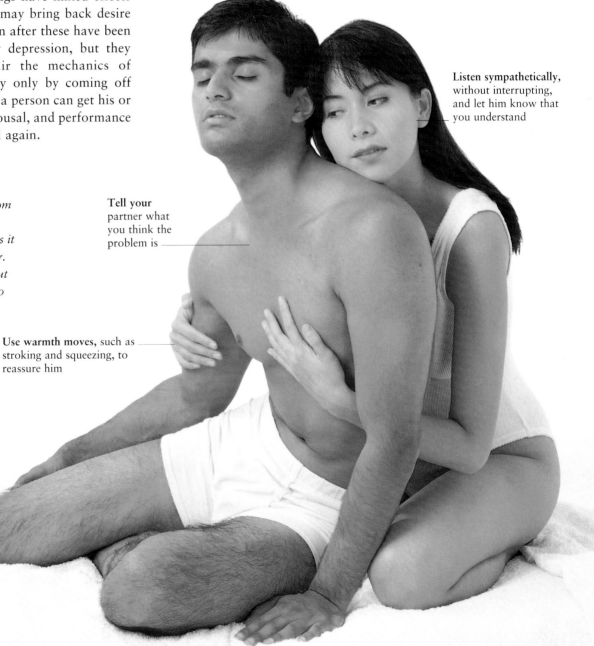

Listen sympathetically, without interrupting, and let him know that you understand

Tell your partner what you think the problem is

Use warmth moves, such as stroking and squeezing, to reassure him

FEMALE SENSATION BLOCKERS

Not nearly enough research has been carried out into women's sexual problems. Some, such as those caused by illness, are well researched. Others, especially those that might have hormonal causes, have yet to be investigated as thoroughly as they deserve, but most sex researchers now agree that hormone imbalances may well be a cause of sexual difficulties.

Ask your partner to allow you time to explain your feelings

The hormone oestrogen, in the right balance, is responsible for a woman's sense of well-being. It keeps the skin moist and the skin texture firm. If natural oestrogen dwindles, the skin dries out and becomes less elastic. Intimate touch, which formerly was pleasurable, may become irritating or even painful in places. The vagina is among the areas directly affected, and it may lose enough moisture and elasticity to make intercourse difficult without adequate additional lubrication, and make orgasm hard to experience.

Testosterone, which women possess in much smaller amounts than men, provides (we think) the ability to experience sexual sensation and sexual desire. Should the amount of free-ranging testosterone circulating in the blood dwindle, women lose interest in sex, may not be so eager to be touched, and find it harder to climax.

Another problem is that high levels of the hormone prolactin, which is secreted during breastfeeding, can sometimes persist after nursing has ceased. High levels of prolactin are responsible for weight gain, general tiredness, and loss of interest in sex. If you experience persistent loss of sexual sensation, please ask your doctor to consider carrying out hormone tests.

ILLNESS

Most of the illnesses that affect male sexual sensation *(see page 128)* will also affect women's ability to feel sensual, but there are some illnesses that women are more prone to. Older women who have not been on hormone replacement therapy (HRT) may find that their joints ache and, later, that they suffer from osteoporosis, or "brittle bones". "Dowager's

TALK IT THROUGH
If a medical or emotional problem is impairing your enjoyment of sex, discuss it honestly with your partner.

hump", the characteristic stoop caused by the crumbling of the top of the spine, is one result of this condition.

Pain in arthritic hips, although not exclusively a female preserve, is much more common in women with osteoporosis, and pain in the joints makes the activity of lovemaking difficult and unpleasant. If a woman begins HRT in her mid to late 40s, it will act as a preventative to osteoporosis (menopause clinics offer advice on HRT). Older women may also find it worthwhile starting HRT because it is known to restore bone density to some extent. It also gives some protection against heart attack.

Just as male sexual activity is made possible by a healthy blood supply to the penis, which ensures erection when the man is sexually aroused, female sexual activity is similarly facilitated. Although research into faulty blood supply to the female genitals is virtually nonexistent, it's reasonable to assume that just as obstructions to the blood supply in this area affect male erection, they are equally likely to impair female sexual response. Arterial dis-

JO AND GENITAL ANAESTHESIA

Jo had a good relationship with her boyfriend, but she couldn't climax. Then one day, when stimulating herself with a vibrator, she noticed that her vagina was contracting. She was having an orgasm, but she couldn't feel it. Jo was one of the small number of women who have perfectly ordinary tactile reactions to touch, but are genitally anaesthetized. We don't know why this should be, but it may be a result of having too little free testosterone in the bloodstream.

ease might be responsible for such obstruction, and so might scar tissue as a result of accidental wounding or surgery.

Studies of diabetic women have shown them to be free of sexual problems, provided that their diabetes is well controlled. They are, however, more prone to vaginal infections such as thrush, which can make intercourse uncomfortable. And, of course, sexual infections of any sort disrupt a good sexual experience and always need prompt medical treatment.

THE EFFECTS OF SURGERY

Anaesthesia and the shock of surgery may cause depression, which in turn lowers desire for sex. Talking feelings through and linking the operation with other life events can help the patient to emerge from the depression, but in most cases it lifts spontaneously anyway. Some radical surgery such as mastectomy or stoma surgery may prove extremely depressing to the individual, but loving touch can do a great deal to restore good spirits and good sensation.

Ovariohysterectomy (removal of the uterus, fallopian tubes, and ovaries) has a more extreme sexual effect. Regardless of age, women experience its after-effects as the menopause, and this may be accompanied by all the classic signs,

including vaginal dryness. Hormone replacement therapy (HRT) and oestrogen cream for the vagina can be a great help.

Depression, as stated, inhibits sexual desire. Manic depression in its manic state often greatly exaggerates sexuality, leading to promiscuity. Drugs and psychotherapy are both valuable. The drugs used to treat schizophrenia affect sexuality, although the condition itself does not.

Vaginal surgery, vaginal tears during childbirth and their subsequent repair, and surgery affecting the rectum may all inhibit perineal blood supply, with the side-effect of reducing sexual response. Poor episiotomy repair after childbirth can make intercourse painful, but can be remedied by surgery to cut out the scar tissue.

The Sexual Effects of Drugs

The adverse effects of drugs such as alcohol on sexual performance are well known, but a great many of the medicines prescribed for common medical problems can have unwanted sexual side-effects. In addition, while some medicines may not possess any unpleasant side-effects (sexual or otherwise) when taken on their own, side-effects may appear if these drugs are combined with alcohol or with other medicines. It is vital, therefore, that you check all drug usage beforehand with your doctor or pharmacist. This is an especially important precaution to take if you intend using any over-the-counter preparations in conjunction with your prescription drugs.

Alcohol

Small amounts may increase sexual desire by reducing anxiety and loosening inhibitions. Moderate amounts can impair a man's ability to achieve or sustain an erection and may prevent him from ejaculating; chronic alcohol abuse can make a man impotent.

Antidepressants

Monoamine-oxidase inhibitors (MAOIs), including pargyline hydrochloride, phenelzine *(Nardil)*, nialamide

These drugs can impair sexual function in a small percentage of users. Some women may experience a decrease in sexual desire and difficulty achieving orgasm; men may develop erection problems, and pargyline can also cause delayed ejaculation.

Tricyclics, including clomipramine hydrochloride *(Anafranil)*

An increase in sexual desire often results from the lifting of depression, but some people find that these drugs make them less interested in sex. Men may also experience erection and ejaculation problems, and some women may find that their ability to achieve orgasm is impaired.

Fluoxetine hydrochloride *(Prozac)*

This is very likely to cause impaired orgasmic ability in women and ejaculation problems in men.

Antihistamines

Histamine H_1-receptor antagonists (in travel sickness, hay fever, and cough remedies), including diphenhydramine hydrochloride *(Benadryl, Benylin)*

Sexual desire may be reduced, and some women experience impaired vaginal lubrication.

Histamine H_2-receptor antagonists (in ulcer-healing preparations), including cimetidine *(Cimetidine, Tagamet)*

Sexual desire may be reduced, and some men experience erection problems.

Anti-Parkinsonism drugs

Levodopa *(L-dopa, Brocadopa, Larodopa)*

Sexual desire may increase.

Blood-lipid control drugs

Clofibrate *(Atromid-S)*

Sexual desire may be reduced, and some men experience problems in achieving erection.

Blood-pressure control drugs

Centrally acting drugs, including methyldopa *(Methyldopa, Aldomet, Dopamet)*

These can cause a decrease in sexual desire, especially at high dosages; these may also lead to erection and ejaculation problems for men, and decreased ability to orgasm for women.

Alpha-blockers, including prazosin hydrochloride *(Hypovase)*; beta-blockers, including propranolol hydrochloride *(Propranolol, Inderal)*; vasodilators, including hydralazine hydrochloride *(Hydralazine, Apresoline)*

Some people find that their sexual desire is reduced, and men sometimes also experience erection problems.

Cannabis

Reports of the sexual effects of small amounts are very subjective and difficult to quantify, but one of the main effects of the drug appears to be an enhancement of the user's state of mind. For example, if you are feeling tired, it will send you to sleep; if you are feeling sexy, it can make you feel more so. The effects of heavy long-term use are more serious but usually disappear quickly when consumption ceases. Effects include a drop in the amount of the sex hormone testosterone circulating in the blood, leading to decreased sexual desire; impotence and impaired sperm production (men); and impaired ovarian function (women).

COCAINE

Small amounts may increase sexual desire and enable men to delay orgasm, but prolonged heavy use can lead to sexual dysfunction in both men (impotence) and women (orgasmic failure).

DIURETICS

Thiazides, such as bendroflumethiazide *(Bendro-flumethiazide, Bendrofluazide, Aprinox, Berkozide, Neo-NaClex)*
Sexual dysfunction may affect a small percentage of people taking these drugs: desire may be reduced, some women experience impaired vaginal lubrication, and some men develop erection problems.
Loop diuretics, such as frusemide *(Frusemide, Furosemide, Diuresal, Lasix)*; potassium-sparing diuretics, such as spironolactone *(Spironolactone, Aldactone, Spirolone)*
These drugs can cause a decrease in sexual desire, especially at high dosages; such dosages may also lead to erection problems for men and decreased vaginal lubrication for women.

HORMONAL PREPARATIONS

Anabolic steroids, such as nandrolone, stanozolol
Misuse of these drugs can cause a number of sexual problems, some of which are serious. In men, these include a drop in the amount of the sex hormone testosterone circulating in the blood, leading to decreased sexual desire; shrinkage of the testicles; impaired sperm production; and growth of the breasts. Women may grow facial and body hair and develop male-pattern baldness, and experience menstrual and ovulation problems and enlargement of the clitoris. Steroid misuse can also trigger rapid mood swings, increased aggressiveness ("roid rage"), and psychosis.
Androgens, such as testosterone preparations
These drugs may help to restore sex drive and orgasmic ability in both men and women. However, high doses

of androgen preparations may cause masculinization in women and suppress sperm production in men.
Anti-androgens, such as cyproterone acetate
Reduced sexual desire may occur in both men and women; men may also experience erection and ejaculation problems and impaired sperm production.
Oestrogens
These hormones may improve vaginal lubrication in post-menopausal women, but in men they can cause loss of sexual desire and serious erection and ejaculation problems.
Oral contraceptives
The effects appear very variable: some women find that sexual desire decreases, others that it increases (perhaps because these drugs ensure that intercourse does not lead to pregnancy).

NARCOTICS

Diamorphine hydrochloride *(heroin)*, **methadone hydrochloride** *(methadone, Physeptone)*
Short-term use can lead to decreased sexual desire, and addiction in men often leads to impotence, ejaculation problems, and sterility. Female addicts may lose the ability to orgasm.

SLEEPING PREPARATIONS

Barbiturates, such as butobarbitone *(Soneryl)*
No adverse effects occur when these are taken for limited periods. Long-term addiction causes loss of sexual desire in women and erection problems in men, sometimes leading to impotence.
Non-barbiturates, such as nitrazepam *(Nitrazepam, Mogadon)*
Most people experience no adverse effects.

TRANQUILLIZERS

Benzodiazepines, including lorazepam *(Ativan, Lorazepam)*, chlordiazepoxide *(Chlordiazepoxide, Librium)*, diazepam *(Diazepam, Valium)*, clorazepate dipotassium *(Tranxene)*
Sexual desire may be reduced; some men experience ejaculation problems, and some women find that their ability to orgasm is impaired.
Phenothiazines, such as chlorpromazine hydrochloride *(Chlorpromazine, Largactil)*; butyrophenones, such as benperidol *(Anquil)*
Sexual desire is often reduced; some men experience ejaculation problems, and high dosages may cause erection difficulties.

EROTIC ENCOUNTERS

You and your partner can often greatly
enhance the eroticism of a sexual encounter by
using fantasy or by creating feelings of, for
example, vulnerability and uncertainty or
dominance and submission. The risk of
discovery and consequent embarrassment can
also add excitement to a lovemaking scenario.

EROTIC ENCOUNTERS

The following pages contain detailed suggestions for unusual and imaginative sexual scenarios that you may enjoy reading and thinking about. You might even like to act them out, either in the way that I've described or in your own versions of them. But if you do choose to act them out, do nothing that is against your partner's wishes or that is likely to harm or embarrass yourself, your partner, or other people.

These scenarios are, of course, only suggestions. They are not carved in stone, and they are not royal commands – they are ideas that may or may not trigger your imagination. Most of them are based on actual sexual fantasies that have been related to me in over 20 years of work as a sex educationalist.

THE NEED FOR INSPIRATION

One of the arguments against sex manuals is that they tell you what to do instead of leaving sex up to your own imagination. It's a strong argument, because few of us like to feel that we have no freedom of choice or that we are being manipulated. But I learned, when running my women's groups many years ago, that some people's imaginations don't work in the same way as others' do. There are men and women who are brilliant, for example, at solving complex abstract problems at work but who haven't a clue where to begin when it comes to varying their lovemaking. They do, however, know enough about life and love to know when a relationship needs something extra. It is these people who seek out guidance and inspiration by reading about sexual fantasies or scenarios, and they often find that the advice given in books such as this one helps them to revitalize their sex lives.

The scenarios that follow are starting points for your imagination, rather than definitive instructions. They may appeal to you in their entirety, they may provide the basis for a good idea, or they may convince you that you're quite happy with what you have. The choice of whether or not to make use of them, in whole or in part, is entirely yours.

GUIDED FANTASY

One easy but effective way to use these descriptions of erotic encounters is in the form of guided fantasy. This is a technique that can involve non-sexual as well as sexual fantasy, and which can be used as a prelude to massage as well as to lovemaking.

One of my most memorable tactile experiences was in San Francisco in the mid-1970s, at the hands of the wonderful massage teacher, Ray Stubbs. He treated me to an exceptional massage that lasted for hours, and which he prefaced by taking me through a guided fantasy. I lay clothed on the massage couch while Ray sat cross-legged at my side and told me a story. He was unhurried, and afterward asked me to describe to him what I'd visualized.

The story itself was very simple. It was my imagination that took wings and soared. He asked me to visualize myself in another country (which I instantly interpreted as another planet), walking along a beach and looking at the sand. To the side of the beach were trees and undergrowth, and my journey took me through these and into the interior. My vision of this scenario was of purple sand and towering orange

mountains nearby – an alien landscape. The trees and the dense undergrowth were tropical and brilliantly coloured, with exotic birds perched among them. As I walked through the forest toward the mountains, bright orange sand swept down from them in rolling dunes, and soon I found myself in a hot desert.

I can't remember much more of this walk, but it doesn't really matter. What I've recounted here gives you the picture. It wasn't erotic, and it wasn't a sexual fantasy: it was a wonderful walk through an unknown landscape, and it created a context for the massage that followed, which felt very nearly out of this world.

Guided fantasy is an experience we can all share, although it's one for special occasions. If you subjected your partner to a guided fantasy every time you gave a massage or made love, the experience could become tedious. But once in a while – that's different! Of course, any plot will do. The secret is not to embellish it yourself – it's your partner who will fill in the details, in his or her mind.

Fears about Fantasy

One of the greatest fears about encouraging the ability to fantasize is that of the fantasy somehow taking over. Many people are afraid that they may end up doing something violent and dangerous, yet that fear is actually their safeguard – it functions as a safety mechanism and prevents them from going any further than they should.

People who end up as killers or violent sex attackers invariably do so because their minds are disturbed, not because of their ability to fantasize. By exploring an idea in your mind you are less likely to go "over the top", because you will have foreseen the consequences.

STARTING POINTS
The scenarios that follow are starting points for your imagination rather than definitive instructions.

Caress your lover's skin with your lips and tongue

Experiment with foods of different flavours and textures

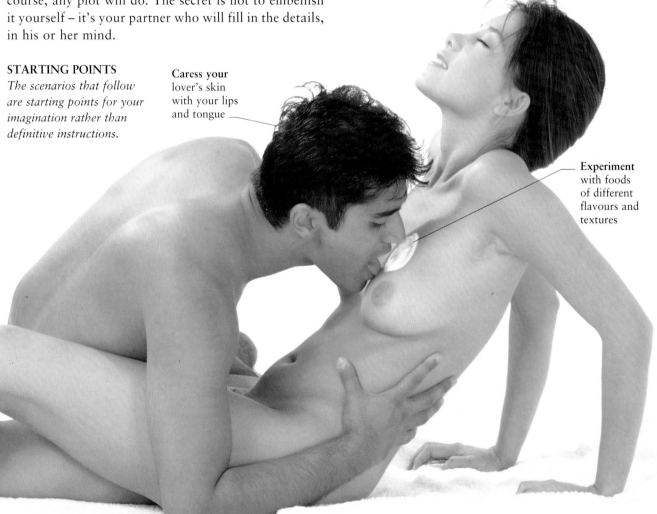

*H*ELPLESS LOVER

The secret of really erotic lovemaking lies in the imagination, and the scenario that follows is a tantalizing example of how you can get your partner's mind racing with expectation. This kind of game, however, should be played only if you have complete trust in each other. Avoid it if either of you has any doubts: it is a bad idea to surrender yourself to someone if you are unsure of the outcome.

Since much of the essence of erotic imagination can lie in the unexpected or in novelty, it would be best if you could afford to book into a hotel room to play this game. If you can't, borrow a friend's apartment for the afternoon. In the description that follows, the man is the helpless lover, but almost exactly the same moves can be made with the woman in that role.

SETTING THE SCENE

Creating a mood of suspense by establishing that you are totally in charge is important. This means that you should visit the room shortly beforehand to prepare it. If you are using a hotel, you should already have

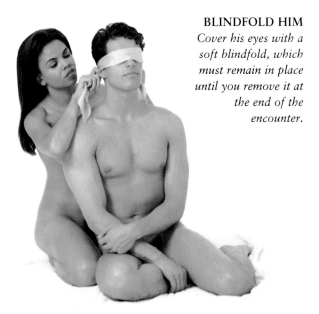

BLINDFOLD HIM
Cover his eyes with a soft blindfold, which must remain in place until you remove it at the end of the encounter.

booked yourself in, acquired a key, set up the room, and put the "Do Not Disturb" sign on the door. Pay attention to small but important details: prepare the bed, set the lighting to how you want it, make sure the room is at a comfortable temperature and the curtains are already drawn, and, if possible, provide music and incense to enhance the atmosphere. You will also need a supply of ice cubes, a flask of hot tea or coffee, a pair of silky boxer shorts (for him), a hairbrush, a piece of velvet, and a piece of silk.

On the way there, you can increase his feeling of uncertainty by refusing to tell him where you are going. Tell him that part of the experience is that he must do whatever you tell him to do (if he feels over-anxious, you can agree on a code word for him to use when he wants you to stop the game). If you are driving to the hotel or apartment, make him drive.

TRICKS AND TREATS

Do not tell him what to expect. Once you are at the apartment or just inside the hotel room, put a blindfold on him, making it clear that in no circumstances is he to remove it. Leave him standing, ordering him not to move, while you go into another room. Let him wait, on his own, for as long as 15 minutes. He will pass through a variety of moods during that time, typically impatience, boredom, anger, and some anxiety. Even though he will suspect that you intend to play all kinds of tricks on him, he won't actually know what is happening. Already, he will be growing emotionally aroused, and that emotional arousal will soon lead to sexual arousal. When you return to the room, tell him to take his clothes off. Then help him put on a pair of soft, silky boxer shorts and tie his hands lightly together with a soft cord. It doesn't matter if the tie is so loose that he could get free if he tried: the point is that he will understand he is being restrained. If there is a bedpost, you can attach the other end of the cord to it. Fondle him through his silky underwear, and if he makes the slightest move to break free, remind him immediately that should he do so, everything stops.

Now put some ice cubes in your mouth for about five to ten seconds, then spit them out and give him oral sex. Stop after a while and drink a couple of mouthfuls of hot coffee or tea to make your mouth hot. Then give him oral sex again. Continue with this alternately hot and cold oral sex for a while, then ask him if what you are doing feels good. When he say yes, leave the room again. He will find this both confusing and provocative, and will probably get annoyed, which is what you're aiming at.

When you return, untie his hands, push him back onto the bed, and give his nipples some attention, licking, sucking, and gently biting them. Then pull his shorts down to his ankles, and use your hairbrush to brush his body hair very slowly down toward his genitals. Brush his pubic hair, too, before pulling his shorts back up and wedging them underneath his genitals. This will make him feel that his genitals are exposed and vulnerable.

Now take your piece of velvet and rub it teasingly over his chest, abdomen, and genitals, and repeat this caress with your piece of silk. Then, still holding the silk, stimulate his penis with it, using some of the

HEIGHTENED AROUSAL
His arousal will be increased by a feeling of helplessness, created by a combination of his nakedness and his inability to see what you are doing.

Unselfish Pleasure

Before you play this game with your lover, you need to accept that it is solely for the benefit of whoever is taking the passive role. When you take the active part, you should expect little out of it except the delight of seeing the pleasure it will give to your partner.

When you are in the passive role, your task is to accept the pleasure that is offered to you. Do not offer your partner any touch, of any kind, in return for what he or she is giving you.

genital massage strokes *(see pages 94-5)*. When he gets an erection and looks as though he's really enjoying your dexterity, stop, saying nothing. Ignore any pleas from him for you to continue or to explain what you are doing, and wait until his erection begins to subside before continuing the genital massage. Repeat this stop-and-start routine, gradually increasing the amount of stimulation you give him, until he climaxes. It is only then, when he has climaxed, that you may take the blindfold off him.

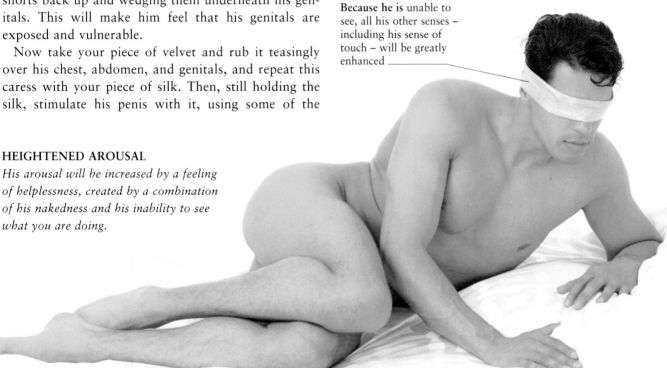

Because he is unable to see, all his other senses – including his sense of touch – will be greatly enhanced

THAI SOAPSUD MASSAGE

Far from Western shores, in lands where the air is hot and humid, it's easy to get the feeling that anything goes, and it often does. Among the many aspects of sex for sale in Bangkok, the capital of Thailand, is total body manipulation lubricated by soapsuds. This very erotic massage is usually given by a woman to a man, but in the right circumstances it can also be given by a man to a woman.

This is a massage that involves a lot of soapsuds and water, so it is best carried out in a large, comfortable bathroom. Much of the preparation is the same as that for the sensual massages described earlier *(see page 64)*, but to evoke the conditions of steamy Thailand, the room should be hot and humid. In addition to a suitable bathroom, you will need a plastic airbed or inflatable mattress, and a good-quality soap or body shampoo that will produce large amounts of long-lasting lather.

MASSAGE FOR HIM

To give your man a Thai soapsud massage, first prepare a warm bath for him and then undress him (he should do very little to help). When he is in the bath, take your own clothes off, wrap yourself in a towel, and bathe him. Soap him lovingly, lathering and gliding your hands over every fraction of his body, including his shoulderblades, his navel, and his genitals. When you reach his feet, slide your fingers into the gaps between the toes and pull each one in turn.

When the washing is finished, ask him to relax in the warm water while you position the airbed next to the bath. Then take your soap or body shampoo and work it up into masses of lather, like pointed peaks of

MAKING SUDS
Use a good-quality soap or body shampoo that produces masses of long-lasting suds.

meringue, and cover the entire surface of the airbed with them. Once the airbed is covered in suds, ask him to step from the bath and lie on his front on the airbed. Heap peaks of suds upon his back, take your towel off, and coat the front of your body with suds.

Next, kneel at your partner's side, then lie on top of him with your well-soaped belly against his back. Slide your body all over him, pushing and wriggling up and down and from side to side, then diagonally from his left buttock to his right shoulder and back again, and from his right buttock to his left shoulder. When you have skated across every inch of his back, use your arms to propel your movements and rub your abdomen backward and forward across his buttocks, pressing his belly and genitals into the airbed. Use regular movements up and down, slow and then fast, so as to give a definite rhythm to the massage strokes.

When you judge that he has had enough stimulation to his back, ask him to turn over. Lather his front with soapsuds, coat yourself with more lather, and lie on top of him again. Sliding back and forth, insinuate your breasts, abdomen, and thighs into every nook and cranny of his front, brushing his genitals but, for a while, keeping clear of his inevitable erection. Now begin teasing him. Slide up and down his body, letting your genitals touch his poised penis on every downstroke and allowing your

Sensual Slipperiness

If the two of you lose slipperiness during the massage, apply more lather. You can, of course, use copious amounts of massage oil instead of soapsuds, drenching your bodies with streams of it so that sliding around on each other is easy. It won't, however, be as visually striking as using suds.

vagina to be penetrated – but only just. As your downward strokes continue, push down on his penis just a little harder each time, so that more and more of it is enclosed until it is in as far as it will go.

This is not yet the moment to begin ordinary sexual intercourse. Focus instead on the whole-body sensation, reversing the previous strokes by gradually lifting off his penis a little on each upward stroke until, once again, you are tantalizing him by just brushing the tip. This process of working down onto his penis, and then up again, can continue for as long as you have the energy and he has the interest. Then, when you judge that the time is right, move faster and bring him to orgasm.

MASSAGE FOR HER

The version of the soapsud massage for a woman is much the same as that for a man, and if both partners are roughly the same weight it will give the same amount of pleasure. Common sense tells us, however, that if your man is twice your weight, it isn't going to work, so don't try it. The lead-in is identical to that of the man's massage, except that the roles are reversed. So also is the sliding over her body, but if either partner is worried about him being too heavy, it might feel safer if he slides up and down along her body instead of moving from side to side, because her entire body frame will support his weight better than only a portion.

SOAP YOURSELF
After you have heaped peaks of suds upon his back, take your towel off, coat the front of your body with suds, and begin the massage itself.

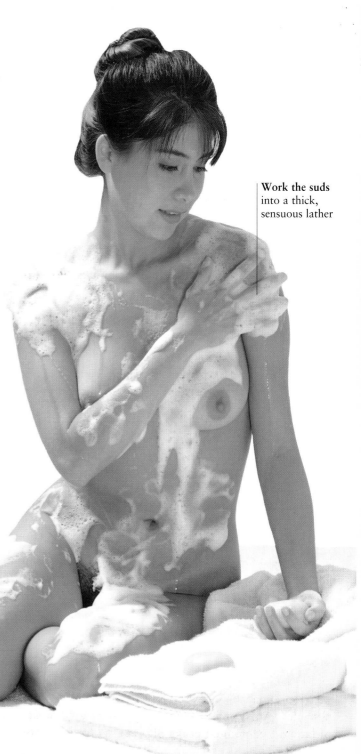

Work the suds into a thick, sensuous lather

141

QUEEN AND SERVANT

When offering an "erotic encounter" to an inhibited female partner, knowing just how far to go can be difficult. One solution is to set up a lovemaking session where you do nothing unless it is specifically requested. But if she is really inhibited, it may be very hard for her to admit to wanting anything, and the result is deadlock. You must overcome this if you want the physical side of your relationship to blossom.

One of the principles of any erotic encounter is that it should be different from an ordinary lovemaking session. It must be set up as a special occasion, but while experienced, confident individuals might welcome being invited to an afternoon or night out at a mystery hotel, strange hotel rooms can feel unpleasantly pressurizing to women who feel uncertain. This doesn't mean that there should be no special preparation, but the occasion may feel more relaxed in the context of your home or hers. Also, tuning in to her mood at the beginning of an evening together is vital.

Setting the scene therefore means thinking about what she would like, rather than what you would like. The kind of scenario described by women in my sexuality groups ranged from lovemaking on a sheepskin rug in front of a roaring fire on a winter's day, to experimenting with sex aids in a way neither partner had ever done. Let's assume that on this occasion it is the sheepskin rug scenario. Draw the curtains, light the fire, take the phone off the hook (or turn down the volume on your answering machine) and make sure that the champagne is within easy reach – a little of it helps to reduce inhibitions. Wear loose, comfortable clothes and begin by just cradling her in your arms.

EASY BEGINNINGS

There is no hurry to this occasion – you might sit for an hour or more, just relaxing and talking. Give her time to unwind and let her lead the way. If it takes more than one session for her to lose her fears and tensions, let it take that time. Show affection by touching

UNDRESSING
When she becomes aroused, you may both want to slip your clothes off so that you can become more intimate.

her lovingly as you talk, for example by nuzzling into her neck and kissing her on the side of her mouth. If she turns her mouth toward you when you do this, kiss her all around it, then lightly on the lips. Take things gently and wait to see how the kissing develops, rather than try to force the pace with too much passion. Above all, do not grope, and do not make a beeline for her sexual parts. Arouse her through warmth, friendship, and by use of the upper half of your body.

When she becomes unmistakably aroused, and your instinct is that she will adore having some special spot (such as her clitoris) stimulated, begin on it gently. If she really doesn't want to be touched there, she's more than likely to shy away from your fingers, and that is your cue to return to arousing her more generally.

But if she welcomes your touch, then suggest that you play a little game. She is a queen and you are her servant, and you may do nothing without her permission. So although you will initiate the moves *(see right)*, she will decide whether to accept or reject them. After you have begun each move, ask her to decide on it by saying, "Does the queen accept or reject this stroke?" The game will work only if you totally accept her rejection of a move: don't argue about her decision, or try to change her mind: just go on to the next one.

SHOW OBEDIENCE
In this game, she is a queen and you are her obedient servant. You may do nothing without her permission.

Moves You Might Make

- Genital massage *(see pages 92–3)*
- Perineal massage – manipulate the sensitive skin between the vagina and anus
- Use one hand to stimulate her clitoris and the other to caress her breasts and nipples
- While stimulating her genitals with one hand, rub the forefinger of the other hand into the gaps between her toes

She is in control, and you are not allowed to question her decisions

Gently kiss her wrist and then work up toward her shoulder

PIANO TEACHER

In bygone days, the storyteller used to be the entertainer of the family or community. It was he (or she) who, by the use of imagination, transported his listeners from the drudgery of everyday life to other times and other lands. Even today, plain old-fashioned storytelling still holds power. Adult story-telling, when the story is a sexual fantasy, can transport you and your partner to a world full of exciting sensual delights.

How you use your sexual story is entirely up to you. For many people, it's enough to have amazing and imaginative suggestions poured into their ears while their lovers stimulate them in every possible manner. Some enjoy having a story read out to them; others like suggesting where their interests lie and encouraging their partners to prepare sexual surprises for them along the lines of the story.

SIMULTANEOUS SEDUCTION

Janet's preference was for the sexual surprises. For some years, she had conjured up sexual fantasies of being dominated and spanked. Indeed, she had devised detailed scenarios involving this, but she kept them

CHOICE OF MUSIC
If neither of you has a piano, base the encounter on some other musical scenario, such as a singing lesson.

strictly to herself and did not dare to disclose them to her new lover, a musician called Roger. But she did let on that she had a particular fantasy of being spanked and seduced simultaneously. Roger took the hint and came up with the goods. His idea worked very well, because he had thought it out like a story beforehand. Here's Janet's account of what happened.

"The great thing about Roger is that he didn't make a secret of the fact that he enjoyed spanking. He was quite open about it, like no one else I've ever met, and it felt fine to tell him about my liking it, too. Perhaps because Roger was a songwriter, he was good with words. He could talk me into feeling intensely excited, and the first time I climaxed with him was while he was telling me a sexy story. But his stories somehow became something more.

"We had been lovers for a few months, but we weren't living together. One day, he set up a special meeting: I was ordered to report for a piano lesson. I duly arrived at his house, in spite of having no desire for piano tuition. He put out a piece of music and told me to play it. 'For every mistake you make, you'll be punished,' he said, and insisted I start, which was terribly unnerving. Of course, it was mistakes from beginning to end. He was sitting beside me on the piano stool and I could feel the tension mounting.

"At first, I believed nothing would happen. I could, after all, just get up and walk away, but I didn't, and something did happen. 'I think you know you must be punished,' he said. 'Stand up and take off your panties.' Outside the door, his mother was vacuuming the hall. I could not believe what I was doing, but I peeled off my panties.

Analysis of the Scenario

Roger, it seems, had instinctively provided all the ingredients guaranteed to maximize Janet's arousal. He set up a special meeting, he acted out a plot, and he made her nervous by setting her up to fail at the piano. Then he intensified that nervousness by choosing (either wittingly or unwittingly) a time when his mother would be right outside the door.

Roger lulled Janet into a sense of false security by stroking her, so that when he did spank, it was much more of a shock. He also aroused her impatience and anger by taking his time to spank her, so that she was again aroused in another sense. He combined caring – in the form of the comforting he gave her – with the arousal of spanking, so that the two became one in her mind, which was both seductive and exciting. Also, he maintained the character of the stern piano teacher instead of lapsing into his real self, which made it easier for her to feel like an ineffectual pupil and completely at his mercy.

"Next, he told me to bend over his knee, and I did so, feeling terribly vulnerable, especially when he lifted my dress so that my bottom was naked. 'This is a nice little bottom,' he said softly, stroking it with his warm hand. For a moment I thought that was all that was going to happen. He stroked some more and I began to feel hot and bothered, but a little disappointed. This wasn't going to lead to anything else after all.

"My disappointment vanished instantly when he spanked me – hard. It stung, and I gasped with shock and anger. But almost immediately he stroked me gently and lulled me again into believing the punishment was over, which I did – until it happened again. He did this so often that I was soon in a state of quite extraordinary arousal. He eventually stroked my clitoris and I climaxed. I couldn't stop coming even though I was still hanging over his knee and his mother was still bumping the vacuum cleaner around outside. It was a fantasy come alive.

"Perhaps it doesn't sound like much, but it was an amazing turn-on, and because of it our relationship flourished. Roger eventually moved in with me and he's still here, six years later."

SPANKING
Playful spanking can give pleasure to both participants, and the effect can be enhanced by alternating spanking with gentle stroking.

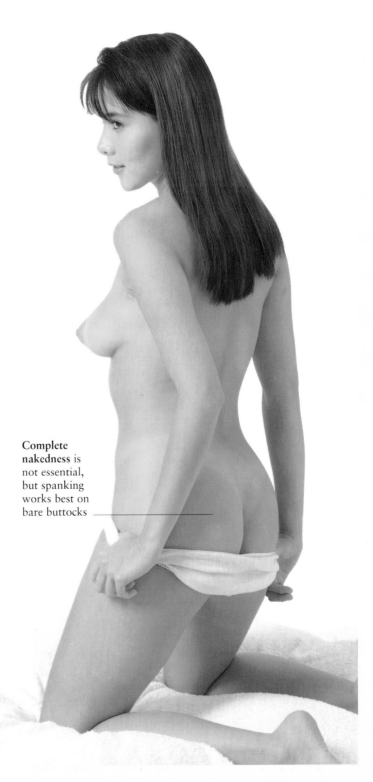

Complete nakedness is not essential, but spanking works best on bare buttocks

FANTASY PICNIC

Some of the most common fantasies are those of exposure, perhaps because many people are closet exhibitionists. Some of the men and women so outwardly shocked by finding they've been watched by a Peeping Tom have, in fact, invited such a viewing. For example, people who undress in front of curtainless windows facing onto the street want to go public, even if they don't fully understand their own behaviour.

The desire to feel exposed may result from a wish to feel vulnerable. There is something about feeling helpless that allows us to enjoy sexuality very fully without experiencing accompanying feelings of guilt. Open-air fantasies often figure in this category, and I vividly remember meeting, in the 1970s, a man who called himself "The Fixer". This man claimed to make other people's fantasies come true.

One of his woman friends, he claimed, had longed to be tied to a tree in a public place and forced to submit to the sexual attentions of any passing male. The Fixer had, he said, set up this dream, only he chose a part of a public forest that was little frequented, and the two men who did stroll by and take advantage were sent

there by him and were not strangers. Today, nobody in his or her right mind would indulge in any kind of casual unprotected sex, and even if multiple sex partners have been arranged by a mutual friend, there is still a health risk involved.

This is where storytelling comes into its own. In a story, we may be subjected to all kinds of indignities but remain safe, and we have the choice of keeping our stories to ourselves and savouring them in isolation, or perhaps getting an extra thrill by hearing them told to us by a lover.

The following is a fantasy recounted to me by Annie, a highly sexed, recently divorced woman, aged 32, who was having difficulty in accepting that her marriage had ended. She had only ever experienced orgasm through masturbation, but did so very easily when pleasuring herself. Although she felt sexually addicted to her ex-husband, he had never stimulated her by hand and she had never liked to ask him to do so.

PICNIC IN THE WOODS

"This is a fantasy I regularly conjured up when I was satisfying myself after John had gone to sleep. In it, I'm at a picnic, in a clearing in the woods. I arrive there with three men – I understand they are friends, even though I don't know them. They are very correctly dressed, in three-piece suits: over-dressed, really, considering that this is a summer's day and a holiday. They all appear to be very respectable. Then with a shock, I realize that I have nothing on. I am completely naked. I cross my hands in front of my breasts, terrified that everyone will see me. But there are only these

SUITABLE FOODS
Squashy foods, such as grapes and other soft fruit, are good ingredients of a fantasy picnic.

three friends. One of them spreads an immaculate damask tablecloth on the ground and pulls the picnic hampers alongside it. Another indicates that I should lie down on it, on my back. He then takes the food from the hampers, and when, after opening the containers, he pours their contents over my body, I begin to understand the part I am to play in this meal.

"Each man drapes a white napkin from his collar and starts to eat the food from my body, as if I am a kind of huge plate. They don't use knives and forks, just their tongues, and quite quickly they work their way through mounds of cream cheese, coleslaw, and slices of pear and banana. Every now and again one of them nips me with his teeth, just to remind me I am quite helpless and have no say in any of this.

"Ultimately there are two men licking cream cheese off my nipples, slowly twirling and sucking them, even chewing on them a little, while the third has poured a great gluey mess of honey down between my legs, and with a raspy tongue is devouring it and me. The mess and the smell, the sense of wetness and stickiness, and the number of men all sucking on me at the same time are overwhelming. Even though I've been told to keep absolutely still, in order to hold the food on my body, I find it quite impossible to prevent my orgasm."

SERVING AND EATING
You can use whichever manner is most appropriate when you are applying the food to your partner's body, but your tongue is the best utensil to use when you are eating it.

Picnic Practicalities

If you want to make a meal of your partner, whether indoors or in the open air, here are some suggestions:
- *Make sure the floor or ground is covered with some waterproof material, such as a plastic sheet, perhaps covered with towels for comfort*
- *Slippery, runny substances work best*
- *A little peppermint toothpaste applied to the nipples or even to the clitoris can give added zest*

Tell your lover what you are about to do, so that she can enjoy the thrill of anticipation

PASSIVE MALE

Contrary to the popular image, a sexually passive man is not a wimp, nor is he unmasculine. He looks like anyone else, he may have a love life like anyone else, and he is probably capable of making love to his partner twice a week in a plain but satisfactory fashion. He does most things expected of a man. But he yearns, usually without even knowing it, to be discovered and seduced by a sexually aggressive woman.

This does not mean that he yearns to be dominated or treated harshly. He wants to be touched suggestively, and tickled and hugged and stroked, but he wants his partner to take the initiative – she has to go there first. He may even be frightened, deep inside, and this fear might cause erection difficulties.

SEDUCING YOUR MAN

It's wise to take time getting close to this man before making any direct sexual advances to him. Spend days on happy outings that have nothing to do with sex. Cuddle and kiss him, but leave it at that. But note how he reciprocates, and if your touch lights him up, if he groans with delight when you range your hands across his body, you will know that he won't mind you taking things further.

The next time you arrange a date, make it casual. For example, you could tell him that you've borrowed a friend's apartment to work in, and that if he'd like to call around at the end of your working day, he'd be welcome. When he arrives, kiss him, keep on kissing him, and allow your bodies to settle on the couch, the floor, even the kitchen table, anywhere as long as you can stretch out, preferably all over him. When his melting body is showing signs of wanting to merge with yours, take his clothes off. Quickly, deftly, remove his shirt, unzip his trousers and strip them off, then take off your own clothes. This just leaves his briefs.

Kissing and biting down the length of his torso, let your hands work their way inside his briefs, then casually peel them off. Now begin oral sex. With your lips covering your teeth, nibble at the sensitive ridge along

TEASING KISSES
Kiss him teasingly on his cheeks, temples, and the sides of his mouth.

the underside of his penis, flutter the tip of your tongue over the head of it, suck on it as though it were an ice cream cone, and swirl your fingers around the base. If he hasn't got an erection when you start these moves, he soon will have.

Next, move up from his genitals and press kisses onto his cheeks, his temples, and the sides of his mouth before allowing your lips to fasten onto his. Run your tongue around the inside of his mouth, and while he is flooded with pleasure and aching with yearning, slide your vagina carefully onto his erection and enclose him tightly. Now drive him on to climax. Pull up above him quite slowly, then thrust firmly down again. You are setting the pace, sending him out of his mind with pleasure and forcing him into a spectacular orgasm.

TAKING THINGS FURTHER

Making love to someone who is passive yet supremely responsive can be addictive. The trouble with this is that it drives you on to take risks. One friend told me that she used to drag her manfriend into dark doorways in remote parts of town and force him to have sex (not that he objected much!). She also gave her lover oral sex while lying in the long grass of a public park, and used to park their car in the same local park, at night, and climb on top of her partner and force him, despite his weak protestations, to perform. But this kind of behaviour is most definitely not recommended. If you want to behave outrageously with your lover, do so in private.

Further Inspiration

If you want to take the initiative and give your partner a sexual treat, here are some suggestions:
- *Give him a genital massage* (see page 94)
- *Treat him to an all-over body grooming where you bath him and towel him dry, as if he were an infant, then shape and shave his body hair*
- *Acquire a mail-order sex-aids catalogue and invest in some wares specially designed for men, then use them on him*
- *Take him to a theme park and put him on the roller-coaster. Aim to make love shortly afterward while the adrenaline is still flowing*

TAKE THE INITIATIVE
He wants you to take the initiative – he will happily follow your lead and emulate your moves, but you have to go there first.

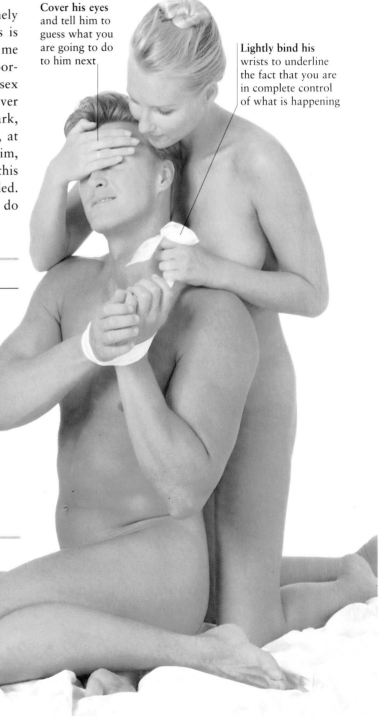

Cover his eyes and tell him to guess what you are going to do to him next

Lightly bind his wrists to underline the fact that you are in complete control of what is happening

ACTING OUT

Our secret sexual desires range from innocent dreams, such as making love by the side of a sparkling lagoon, to sophisticated longings for restraint and domination. Bringing each other's desires to life can bring great pleasure and also create very special mutual trust between lovers.

The following stories are personal accounts of what happened when three people acted out their fantasies with their partners, and they illustrate how inner desires can be made to come true. I must emphasize, however, that if your fantasy is one that involves doing anything that is dangerous or illegal, it is best if you keep it to yourself.

THE MASSEUR

"I arranged to meet my girlfriend at my best friend's apartment during her lunch hour. I didn't tell her my plans, but as soon as I arrived, I put on a white overall and asked her to take her clothes off. Then I gave her a thoroughly professional massage, which she hadn't known I could do. I didn't make it sexual, though. When I was through, I knew very well that she was aroused, and asked, 'Will there be anything else, Madam?'

"She hesitated before replying, 'What else is there?' 'There are special services, Madam, but they cost extra,' I told her. We haggled over the price and then she actually paid me. I gave her a genital special, which resulted in her having an intense orgasm. A minute later she leaped to her feet, saying she had to get back to work, and we left.

"Now, once a month, I give her a session where I stay in character as the masseur and she acts the part of the client. She's become a lot more assertive in this role, and I find myself being asked to do some things I'd never

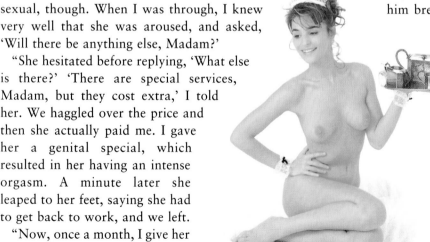

ADDED REALISM
Simple props that reflect the theme of the fantasy will make it more realistic.

have guessed she'd want. The fact that she's paying for it seems to have liberated her in some way, and while the massages feel separate from the rest of our relationship, they have undoubtedly strengthened it."

THE MAIDSERVANT

"I have a fantasy about being a 16th-century serving girl who brings breakfast to the gentlemen of the house in their bedchambers. When I go into each room, I draw back the heavy drapes at the windows, then offer the tray to the man in bed. One of them decides to have his way with me, and as a serving girl, I have to accept whatever he chooses to do.

"My boyfriend knew about the fantasy and took me by surprise one morning. When I brought him breakfast in bed, he put it firmly to one side and told me there was an important part of his appetite that needed to be satisfied first. Before I knew it, he'd tied my hands to the end of the bed, stripped off my pyjama bottoms, and bent me over. Then he quite blatantly used me, making it clear that I would have to put up with this treatment.

"He didn't climax, though. At the last minute, he withdrew. 'I've changed my mind,' he said, and got on with his breakfast. But he didn't untie me, just left me there exposed. I felt a fool. I also felt quite angry, and demanded to be untied. 'I'll untie you,' he said, 'if you agree to lie on your back on the bed and when I've finished my breakfast, let me finish having sex with you.' 'No way,' I spat, 'You must be joking'. 'No,' he said, and left me there. Every ten minutes or so, he'd ask me if I'd changed my mind, and after about half an hour, I realized I'd be staying there all day if I didn't agree to his demands.

"Enraged, I grumpily agreed. What I hadn't expected was that instead of just getting on with what he'd left off, he massaged me erotically all over. I got very turned on in spite of myself and climaxed without meaning to. I realized later that he'd made me angry on purpose, on the grounds that one kind of arousal leads to another. I'm careful about bringing him breakfast in bed now. But I'm not totally averse to the idea!"

THE HOOKER

"I'd heard stories about hookers turning up at their clients' apartments wearing little or nothing under their coats, and often wondered at their daring. Then, one night, my lover had to stay at a hotel near where I lived, because he was attending a conference there. He invited me to visit him, so I took a deep breath and left off most of my clothes, covering my flimsy underwear and stockings with my great-aunt's old fur coat.

"Just walking from the car to the hotel entrance filled me full of adrenaline. And once inside, I was terrified that the receptionist would think I was a hooker, and throw me out. To my relief, if the receptionist thought there was anything strange going on, he didn't show it. When my lover opened the door to his room, I let the coat fall open and he understood immediately what I'd done. He drew me inside and we made love immediately. I had been so nervous I was on fire, and I climaxed almost as soon as he came inside me. The physical thrill of actually living out something I'd fantasized about was incredible."

Keep It Special

The three scenarios that were described here are good examples of how you can inject variety into your sex life. But remember, acting out a fantasy will lose its excitement if it becomes routine – indulge in it sparingly, so that it retains its special qualities.

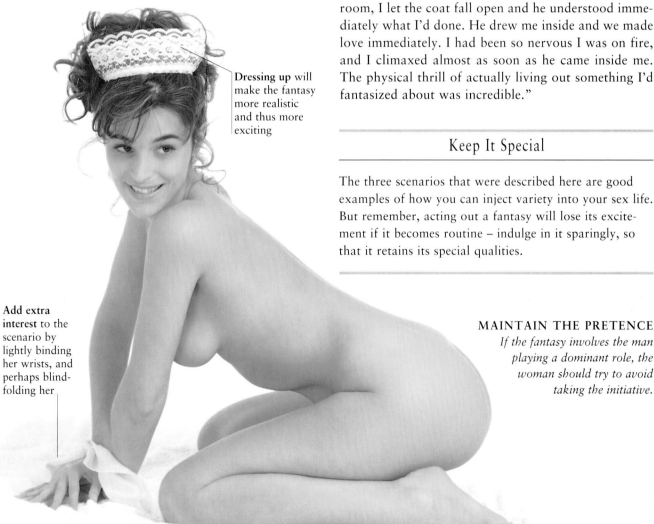

Dressing up will make the fantasy more realistic and thus more exciting

Add extra interest to the scenario by lightly binding her wrists, and perhaps blind-folding her

MAINTAIN THE PRETENCE
If the fantasy involves the man playing a dominant role, the woman should try to avoid taking the initiative.

LISTEN TO MY TAPE

This is another scenario which relies on creating a sense of helplessness and frustration. Total trust is necessary here, because one of you has to agree to obey the other – any game where you put yourself totally into someone else's power is not to be carried out with strangers or with anyone with whom you feel uncertain. If either of you has any doubts about it, stick to plain massage and lovemaking.

Arrange to meet at a borrowed apartment, and be there first to welcome your partner lovingly and affectionately when she arrives (assuming it is she who obeys on this occasion). Ask her to undress and lie down on the bed, then tie her arms and legs with silken ties. Last of all, put a soft blindfold around her head, but make sure that her hearing is unimpeded.

Once she is settled, promise her that great things will happen. Stroke her cheek, give her a loving kiss, and then leave the room. Leave her for 15 minutes – just long enough for her to start getting restless and to wonder what is happening, but not long enough to get really cross. When you return, say something quite maddening, such as, "Oh, are you still here?"

THE TAPE RECORDER

When she demands attention, as she's highly likely to do, it's your cue to say, "Well, I can't attend to you right now – you'd better make do with this," and put down next to her a small cassette-player or personal stereo. Inside it is a 90-minute cassette tape, on one whole side of which you have recorded yourself saying the most suggestive, lecherous, and arousing things you can think of, and outlining what marvellous plans you have for lovemaking.

What she doesn't know, but is going to find out, is how long the tape goes on for. This isn't just a five-minute job – it just goes on and on, for 45 minutes. She, lying on that bed, is completely unable to move, incapable of escaping the voice, or the blindfold, or the silken knots, however much she wants to. And if she is

responsive to your suggestions, she will be desperate to do something about them. But of course, there's nothing she *can* do. When you finally return, she's going to be as angry as she is erotically inflamed. She may threaten you or tell you that you will be very sorry.

This is your cue to ask her what she would like to happen next. Her answer is most likely to be, "Untie me immediately and take the blindfold off!" You may reply, "OK, but when I've released you,

SILKEN TIES
When she has undressed, bind her wrists and ankles firmly but gently with silken cords or silk scarves.

I am going to subject you to all kinds of indignities and you will have to accept them. If you don't agree, there'll be no untying." Your "indignities" will consist of a wonderful erotic massage, performed when she is unbound but still blindfolded.

THE PLEASURE

After massaging her body and limbs, but before beginning any genital strokes *(see page 92)*, tell her that you have to leave the room again briefly, but you are not going to retie her – you are putting her on trust not to move away from the bed. While you are away, she is to listen to the tape again, this time side two on which you describe in graphic detail, stroke by stroke, exactly what you intend to do during the genital massage.

While you are out of the room, quickly change your clothes, put on a cologne or aftershave that you normally never use, then don very thin surgical gloves and coat them with massage oil. When you return to the room to give her the genital massage, don't utter a word – because she is still unable to see, it is quite possible that she will think you are someone else, especially if you have hinted at this possibility at the beginning of the second recording.

When your genital massage brings your lover to orgasm, take off her blindfold and hold her close. You reassure her that you love her and that she can trust you, by cradling her and kissing her. You make it clear, just in case she really thought there might be someone else in the room, that there isn't.

The Emotional Dynamics

In case, after reading this, you are still wondering what precisely has been going on, here is an explanation. With your cavalier behaviour, and by trapping your lover with the inflammatory tape recording, you conjure up many emotions inside her head.

But, you may observe, most of those emotions are frustration and anger. They are indeed, and the longer they continue the more powerful they become. Sexual arousal is close to other strong emotions, as is the ability to fall in love. Psychological tests have shown that we are most likely to fall in love if we have just experienced a shock or a crisis of some kind – our adrenaline levels are increased and so too is our eroticism. By insisting on her agreement and acquiescence, when she is probably very angry, you heighten that arousal as well as her sense of vulnerability.

MIND PICTURES
The blindfold will encourage her mind to create its own pictures and to draw its own conclusions.

Cross her wrists before tying them

Blindfolding her will concentrate her mind on the words she is hearing

SAFER SEX

The term "safer sex" refers to sexual activity that will not lead to the transmission of infection from one partner to the other, especially infection with the human immunodeficiency virus (HIV), the virus responsible for AIDS. Safer sex is generally regarded as sex where there is no exchange of body fluids.

Many people still believe, erroneously, that AIDS is not a heterosexual disease and refuse to take precautions. Others understand the dangers but feel that these are slight, and anyway find it impossible to ask a partner to use a condom or to consider whether or not they might have been exposed to the risk of HIV infection. Then there are the sensible people, who are fearful of getting AIDS and who practice safer sex conscientiously.

Put bluntly, the surest ways to avoid AIDS are by choosing to be celibate; practising sexual activities that do not involve any intercourse; and always using condoms when you do have intercourse, which will give you a significant level of protection against infection.

CONDOMS

For maximum protection against sexual infection – and unwanted pregnancy – condoms must be of dependable quality and used correctly. You should avoid obscure brands and strangely shaped (especially knobbly) sheaths, and check that the use-by date has not passed. Just as importantly, condoms must be used correctly.

Do not unroll a condom as soon as you take it out of the package, because it is almost impossible to use a condom once it has been unrolled. It should be unrolled directly onto the erect penis *(see opposite page)*, and it should be a snug fit, because if it is not tight enough it might slip off the penis or leak semen into the vagina during intercourse. For extra protection against HIV, use condoms that have been treated with the spermicide nonoxynol-9.

LEVELS OF RISK

The following are examples of ways in which you are likely or unlikely to catch HIV from an infected person.

You are likely to get HIV from:
• Intercourse without using a condom
• Fellatio, especially to ejaculation
• Anal intercourse

You are less likely to get HIV from:
• Intercourse using a condom
• Cunnilingus
• Bites and scratches that break the skin

You have a slight risk of HIV from:
• Mouth-to-mouth kissing if either of you has bleeding gums or cold sores

• Sharing sex aids such as vibrators
• Very gentle lovebites or scratches that break the skin

You won't get HIV from:
• Dry kissing
• Wet kissing, as long as neither partner has bleeding gums or cold sores
• Stimulating the body with the hands
• Stimulating the genitals by hand
• Swallowing saliva, if there are no cuts in your mouth
• The bites of mosquitoes, fleas, or other bloodsucking insects
• Sneezes; toilet seats; telephones; other people's beds or towels; swimming pools; sharing food; shaking hands

Some men and women dislike using condoms, but this is a learned aversion that can be unlearned relatively easily. As an alternative to male condoms, try using the female versions, which fit into the vagina rather than over the penis. For protection against infection during oral sex, use oral shields ("dental dams") for cunnilingus and condoms for fellatio; flavoured condoms can make fellatio through a condom more enjoyable for a woman.

PUTTING ON THE CONDOM

Once they have achieved erection, many men produce drops of seminal fluid long before ejaculation, so the condom should always be fitted to the erect penis before you have any genital contact.

To make the fitting of the condom an erotic experience, the woman should treat her lover to a little genital massage, using a water-based lubricant *(see Condom Care above),* before rolling the condom into place on his penis. Apply lubricant sparingly: too much can result in the condom slipping off the penis during intercourse.

When fitting the condom, place it on the tip of the penis and gently squeeze its teat or nipple, if it has one, between thumb and forefinger to expel any air from it. An air bubble in the tip could cause the condom to split during the friction of vigorous intercourse. If the condom has no teat, squeeze its tip to expel air and leave about a centimetre free to collect the semen.

With the condom on the head of the penis and the air squeezed out, hold it in place with one hand and carefully roll it down to the base of the penis with the other. If your partner is uncircumcised, push back his foreskin before adorning him. If the condom turns out to be far too short and doesn't reach the base of his penis, he should not penetrate you past the end of the condom because this can cause it to come off inside you.

If, during intercourse, either of you feels the condom slipping off, one of you can reach down and grasp it at the base of the

CONDOM CARE

If you are using male condoms you must avoid bringing them into contact with oil-based products, including massage oils and creams. Most male condoms are made of latex, and this material is damaged and weakened by contact with oil; within 15 minutes of contact with an oil-based product, a latex condom can lose up to 95 per cent of its strength.

Female condoms are made of polyurethane, which is not harmed by oil-based products; polyurethane male condoms are being developed.

In addition to massage oils and creams, products that can damage latex condoms include baby oil, petroleum jelly (such as Vaseline), hand cream, vegetable oils, margarine, butter, suntan lotions, and some vaginal pessaries and rectal suppositories.

If you need to use a lubricant, choose a reputable water-based product such as K-Y Jelly. If you have been massaging each other, you must wipe any traces of oil, lotion, or cream completely from your hands before handling a condom.

penis to keep it in place. This not only prevents it from slipping off, it also creates some additional pleasurable sensations for your partner. When your man eventually climaxes, he should withdraw from you, holding the condom in place, before his penis loses all its erection. This is so that the condom doesn't slip off and allow semen to leak inside you.

SENSUALIZING THE CONDOM

There are various ways in which you can get used to handling condoms and making the fitting of them more sensual. When you masturbate, try putting a condom on your finger and stimulating yourself with it. Experiment with different-coloured condoms, and with using your mouth to put a condom on to your man's finger. When you get good at that, try it on his penis.

Types of Condom

The male condom is a latex sheath that is rolled on to the erect penis. The female condom is a soft, polyurethane cylinder, closed at one end, that fits inside the vagina.

Male condoms

Female condom

INDEX

FURTHER READING

BANCROFT, JOHN
Human Sexuality and its Problems (2nd edition)
Churchill Livingstone, Edinburgh, 1989

BROWN, PAUL AND FAULDER, CAROLYN
Treat Yourself to Sex
Penguin, London, 1980

DODSON, BETTY
Sex for One: The Joy of Selfloving
Crown Trade Paperbacks, New York, 1987

HOOPER, ANNE
Anne Hooper's Kama Sutra
Dorling Kindersley, London, 1994

HOOPER, ANNE
Anne Hooper's Pocket Sex Guide
Dorling Kindersley, London, 1994

HOOPER, ANNE
Anne Hooper's Ultimate Sex Guide
Dorling Kindersley, London, 1992

HOOPER, ANNE
Massage and Loving
Unwin Paperbacks, London, 1988

HOOPER, ANNE
The Body Electric
Pandora, London, 1991

HOOPER, ANNE
Women and Sex
Sheldon Press, London, 1986

INKELES, GORDON, AND TODRIS, MURRAY
The Art of Sensual Massage
Unwin Paperbacks, London, 1973

KAPLAN, HELEN SINGER
Disorders of Sexual Desire
Balliere Tindall, London, 1979

KINSEY, ALFRED C, AND POMEROY, WARDELL B
Sexual Behavior in the Human Male
W. B. Saunders Company, Philadelphia, 1948

KINSEY, ALFRED C, POMEROY, W B, MARTIN, C E, GEBHARD, P H
Sexual Behavior in the Human Female
W. B. Saunders Company, Philadelphia, 1953

MASTERS, WILLIAM H, AND JOHNSON, VIRGINIA E,
Homosexuality in Perspective
Little, Brown, Boston, 1979

MASTERS, WILLIAM H, AND JOHNSON, VIRGINIA E,
Human Sexual Response
Little, Brown, Boston, 1966

MASTERS, WILLIAM H, JOHNSON, VIRGINIA E,
AND KOLODNY, ROBERT C
Heterosexuality
Thorsons, London, 1994

MONTAGU, ASHLEY
Touching: The Human Significance of the Skin
Harper & Row, New York, 1978

STOPPARD, DR MIRIAM
The Magic of Sex
Dorling Kindersley, London, 1991

STOPPARD, DR MIRIAM
Woman's Body: A Manual for Life
Dorling Kindersley, London, 1994

STUBBS, KENNETH RAY
Romantic Interludes: A Sensuous Lovers Guide
Secret Garden, Larkspur, 1986

ACKNOWLEDGMENTS

Photographic assistance: Nick Allen and Sid Sideris;
additional photographic assistance by Brian Glover. Bath
supplied by The Water Monopoly, metronome and music
stand by Chappell of Bond Street

Hair and make-up: Bettina Graham
Additional hair and make-up by Melissa Lackersteen
and Pip Whiteside

Illustrator: John Geary
Anatomical references by Sandie Hill

Design assistance: Beverly Lagna, Juanita Grout

Production consultant: Lorraine Baird